Marek Studziński

The History of Palestine
From 10,000 BC until 2,024 AD

Philistines – Israel – Jews – Christians – Arabs

For my mum, who has just died.

The History of Palestine

from 2,000 BC to 2,024 AD

as Graph and Table

Migration, mass migration

war

Exile, expulsion, resettlement

Damage to the civilian population

Contents

Introduction

The territory of Palestine is one of the oldest settlement areas of mankind. Jericho is the oldest city in the world. The first settlement dates back to around 10,000 BC.

This piece of land had not had a happy history. Its position between the great powers of Egypt and Assyria is not exactly ideal. Many armies travelled through the country. The country remained under foreign rule and administration for centuries.

The Southern Kingdom of Israel only existed as a sovereign state for around 250 years. That was all. Then it was over and done with. The state of the Philistines or the state of Palestine never existed. They had several city states and formed a loose confederation of cities.

19 different rulers dominated the area! Some of the population was enslaved, deported, murdered and disenfranchised. The decimation, exchange and migration of the population was very high here. Some came, others had to leave. The fluctuations were already very pronounced. The fate of the inhabitants was dramatic and painful. Which great power was the victorious one in retrospect?

The three world religions.

Judaism, Christianity and Islam have left the biggest traces here and are visible everywhere. Jewish, Christian and Islamic religious affiliations are inextricably linked in the region and in the city of Jerusalem.

The table was originally based on the historical book „Historia Żydow w starozytnosci - Od Thotmesa do Mahometa" von Łukasz Niesiołowski-Spanò and Krystyna Stebnicka. The work deals with the history of the Jews up to Mohammed. That was the beginning. The table was later supplemented with additional sources and inserted accordingly.

In the table, it was important to me to describe not only Jews, but also Philistines and Arab groups. This is perhaps the special thing about this elaboration, that several ethnic groups are mentioned. Around 600 BC, the Philistines were exterminated as a people by Nebuchadnezzar. They disappeared forever.

The Old Testament is not regarded as a historical source of history in Palestine. Nevertheless, it is an important indication of how the Jewish elite thought and felt. It talks a lot about the conquest of Palestine, the subjugation of the peoples, the destruction of the cities and the enmity with the Philistines.

Of course, some quotes from the New Testament and the Koran were not to be missed. They are just as much a part of it as historical facts and events.

Finally, some points of the Hamas Charter are presented. This shows how much they regard the Koran as the basis of their lives and how extremely Islamic values are embodied by them. The whole of Palestine should only belong to the Muslims, and they will die and fight for it. The Israelites have no business there. They are not even negotiated with.

That is why I believe that there will be no peace in Palestine. There is more of a religious war going on there.

In its 12,000-year history, the land of Palestine has been home to many inhabitants, many rulers, many peoples, many cultures and many languages. The gods El, Baal and Asherah have lived there since time immemorial, long before the Philistines came to Palestine. God played an important role in this area.

Today it is YHWH, Jesus and Allah who are to share the land peacefully. There were times when 90% of the population were Christians. The State of Israel existed on the territory for only 320 of 4,000 years. That is just under 1% of the time.

Historically, the land belongs to no one exclusively.

> Palestine does not belong to the Jews.

> Palestine does not belong to the Christians.

> Palestine does not belong to the Muslims.

>> Palestine does not belong to YHWH.

>> Palestine does not belong to Jesus.

>> Palestine does not belong to Allah.

The land of Palestine belongs to itself. It endures all its inhabitants; it survives them all. On earth you are only a pilgrim and a traveller. We are not owners. Because everything has its specific and limited time.

According to the Bible, the land of Caan was overrun and defeated by force and without mercy. The conquerors came out of Egypt and the desert in search of a new home for the great people.

A new home! Nobody gives up their property and land voluntarily, so it has to be done with sword and fire.

General Joshua was a successful conqueror and occupier. The Israelites were bloodthirsty and greedy for the foreigner.

The Bible shows an enmity between the Jewish people and other ethnic groups. The antipathy between the Philistines and the Israelites was particularly strong. They were constantly at war with each other. Hatred and anger were in the air. Weapons and beatings were their brutal language.

Under King Solomon, peaceful times are said to have prevailed between the neighbours. That was only short-lived.

Christianity sees Jesus Christ as the true Messiah of the Jews. But he is different from what the Jews imagined him to be. He was peaceful. He did not lead a rebellion or wage war against the Romans. The Jews still reject him today. Jesus plays no role for them, only Moses and the Torah.

The Koran itself speaks of the Prophet Jesus, the son of Mary. They also reject Jesus as Saviour and God. For them, only Mohammed told the truth about God Allah. Islam presents itself as the only true religion. For him, Judaism and Christianity are misconceptions. Muslims have the true faith of Abraham and therefore condemn Jews and Christians as false doctrines. They are also descended from Abraham but have developed in evil directions.

The Jews have 613 rules of life. Christians believe in miracles, the cross, resurrection and the Trinity. That does not exist in the Koran. Islam is much simpler and recognises only five pillars.

If three world religions do not respect but reject each other, how can there be peace in Palestine?

The basis of all freedom is acceptance, not rejection. Antipathy leads to war and expulsion.

The thought of revenge and anger has never brought two parties together.

Jerusalem is a capital city for three world religions. That will never change. There can never be just one winner.

So only together.

God promised Abraham that he would give him the land: "I will give this land your offspring" [Genesis 12:7] In other words, descendants of Ishmael and Isaac. Abraham said, "Praise be to God, who has given me, in my old age, Ishmael and Isaac." [Sure 14, 38-41] Ishmael and Isaac are Abraham's heirs.

Marek Studziński

World religions and Palestine

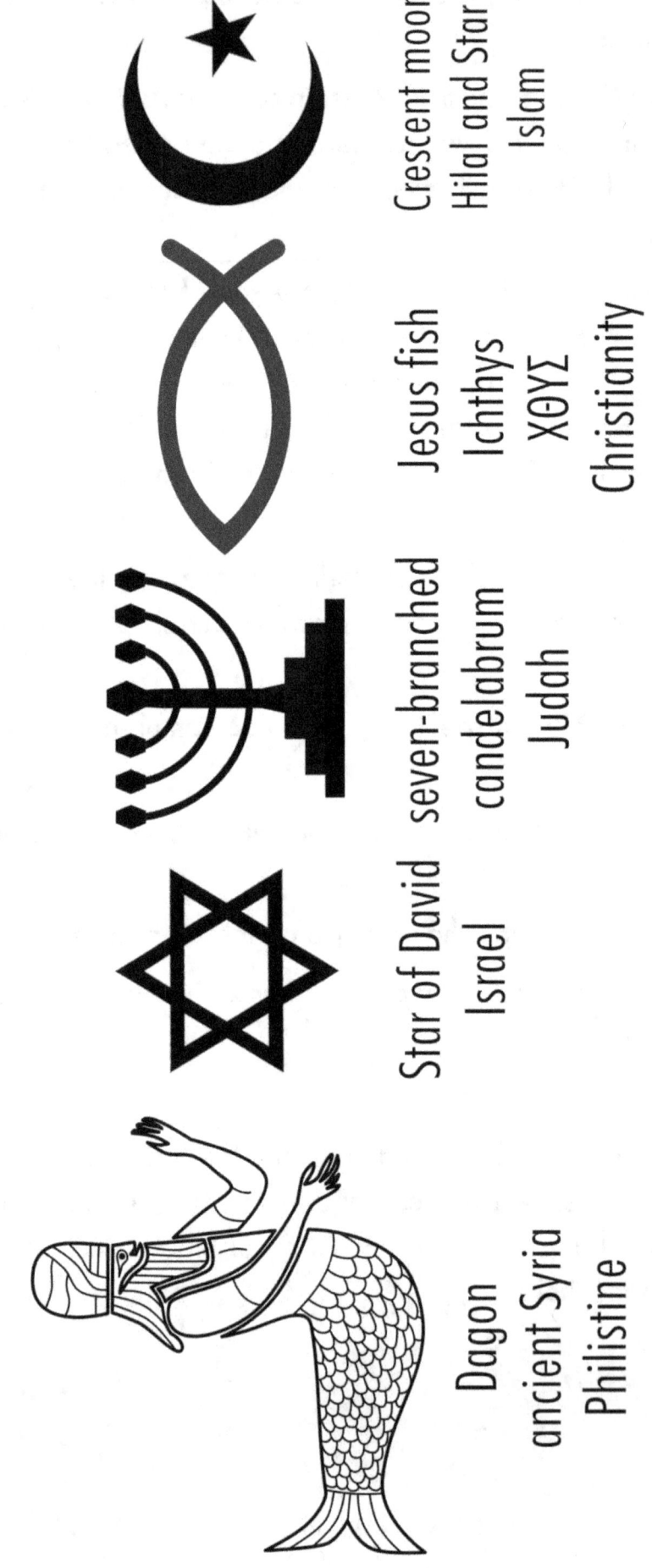

Crescent moon
Hilal and Star
Islam

Jesus fish
Ichthys
ΧΘΥΣ
Christianity

seven-branched
candelabrum
Judah

Star of David
Israel

Dagon
ancient Syria
Philistine

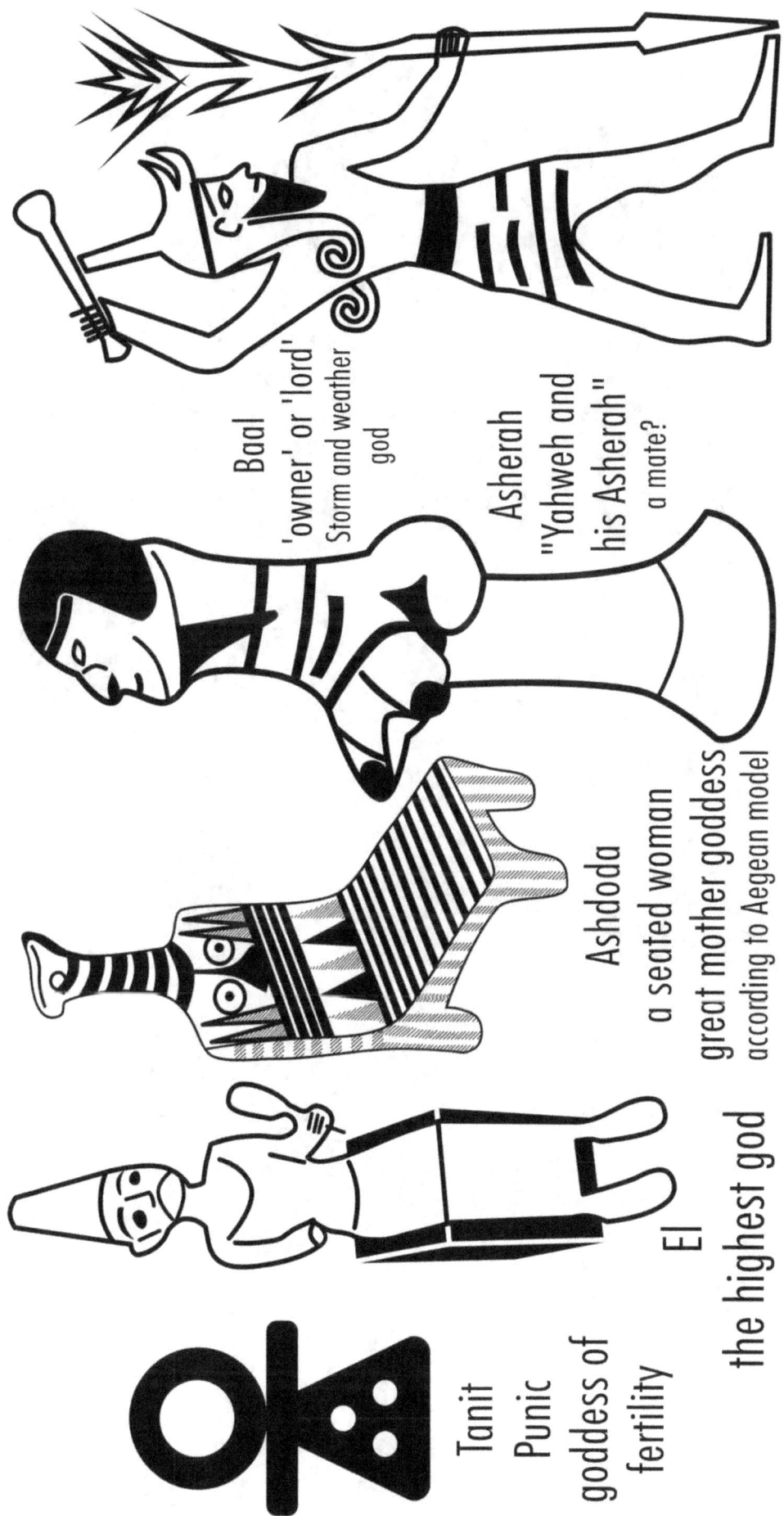

Baal
'owner' or 'lord'
Storm and weather god

Asherah
"Yahweh and his Asherah"
a mate?

Ashdoda
a seated woman
great mother goddess
according to Aegean model

El
the highest god

Tanit
Punic
goddess of fertility

Israel and its Neighbours

Times of rule in Palestine

	Rules	From	Until	Years	Gods
1	Hurrian	2000 bc	1550 bc	450	El, Baal, Asherah
2	Egyptian	1550 bc	1150 bc	400	
3	Philistine	1170 bc	925 bc	245	Ashdoda, Mother Goddess, Dagon
4	Israel	926 bc	734 bc	192	YHWH, Elohim, Adonai
5	Assyrian	734 bc	630 bc	104	
6	Judah	845 bc	586 bc	259	YHWH, Elohim
7	Egyptian	640 bc	604 bc	36	
8	Babylonian	605 bc	539 bc	66	
9	Persian	538 bc	302 bc	236	YHWH, Elohim
10	Hellenistic	330 bc	63 bc	267	YHWH, Elohim
11	Hasmonea	129 bc	63 bc	66	YHWH, Elohim
12	Rom	63 bc	337 ad	400	YHWH, Jesus Christus
13	Byzantine	337 ad	640 ad	303	Jesus Christus, YHWH
14	Arab	636 ad	1099 ad	463	Allah, Jesus Christus, YHWH
15	Crusader	1089 ad	1291 ad	202	Jesus Christus, Allah, YHWH
16	Mamluk	1291 ad	1516 ad	225	Allah
17	Ottoman	1517 ad	1917 ad	400	Allah
18	British	1917 ad	1948 ad	31	Allah, Jesus Christus
19	Israel	1948 ad	2024 ad	76	Allah, YHWH, Jesus Christus

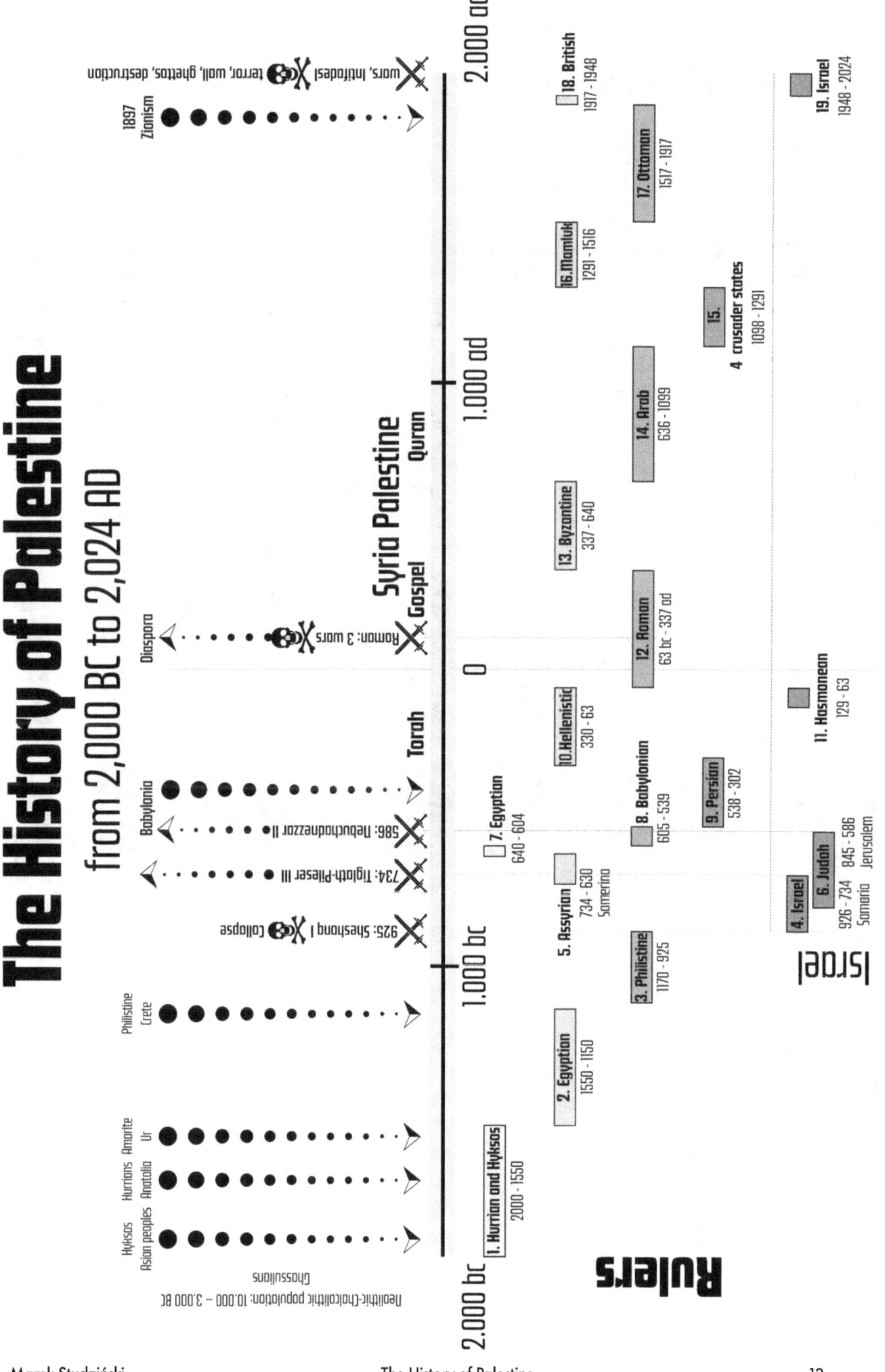

The History of Palestine

from 2,000 BC to 2,024 AD

Soleb and Amara-West	1.360 BC.	"Shasu-**Yahu**" (YHWH)
Stela ('First Stela') of Seti I	1.280 BC.	group of rebellious **Canaanite** towns
Stela of Ramesses II	1.261 BC.	stability of trade routes in the **Canaanite**
Stela ('Second Stela') of Seti I	1.250 BC.	stability of trade routes in the **Canaanite**
Merenptah Stele *Pharaoh Merenptah*	1.208 BC.	"**Israel is** devastated, its seed is no more"
Mesha Stele *King of Moab*	860 BC.	"**Omri**, the king of **Israel**" "the altars of **YHWH**"
Stela Salmanasara III	853 BC.	Enemy **Ahab** from **Israel**
Tel Dan	840 BC.	"House of David"
Kuntillet Ajrud, Khirbet el-Qom	800 BC.	"**Yahweh** and his **Asherah**"
Kuntillet Adschrud	760 BC.	"**YHWH** of Samaria", "**YHWH** of Teman"

Abram

*"I will give this land
to your offspring"*
Genesis 12:7

*"Praise be to God,
Who has given me,
in my old age,
Ishmael and Isaac."*
Sure 14, 38-41

1. Ishmael (Agar)

2. Isaac (Sarah)

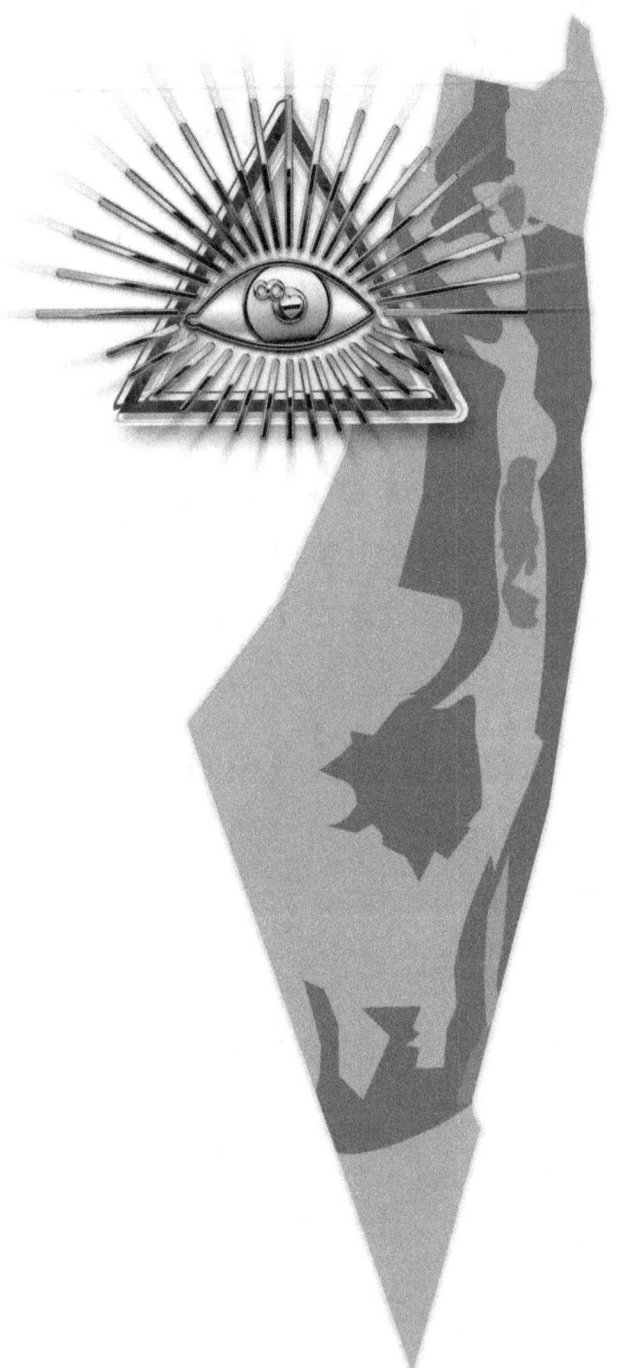

Abram

"I will give this land
to your offspring"
Genesis 12:7

History of Palestine - in tabular Form

	Name Palestine
	The name "Palestine" was originally an adjective derived from Philistia (Peleshet).
	The name is probably derived from the Greek word for "land of the Philistines".
	Hebrew פְּלֶשֶׁת Pleschet - Peleset (Philistine)
	Prst or Plst in ancient Egyptian
	Pilišti, Palaštu in Assyrian sources
	The English term "Palestine" is ultimately derived from "Philistaea".
	"Palestine" means "Land of Pales", after the ancient androgynous deity Pales?
	Blood revenge
	The "eye for an eye" law was intended to curb blood feuds. The right to retaliation is intended to restore family honour by killing an enemy.
1.920 BC.	Codex Ešnunna from Mesopotamia: If a man bites off a man's nose and cuts it off, he pays one mine of silver.
1.792 – 1.750 BC.	Codex Hammurapi: a collection of laws with 282 paragraphs on a stele accessible to the public
250 BC.	Tanach: "An eye must be put out for an eye. A tooth must be knocked out for a tooth. A hand must be cut off for a hand and a foot for a foot. A burn must be given for a burn, a wound for a wound, and a bruise for a bruise." Exodus 21,24-25 "A bone must be broken for a bone. An eye must be put out for an eye. A tooth must be knocked out for a tooth." 3.Moses 24,20
30 AD.	Christus: "'You have heard that it was said, "An eye must be put out for an eye. A tooth must be knocked out for a tooth." But here is what I tell you. Do not fight against an evil person. Suppose someone slaps you on your right cheek." Matthew 5,38-39 "Don't pay back evil with evil. Be careful to do what everyone thinks is right." Roman 12,17
632 AD.	Koran: "a life for a life, an eye for an eye, a nose for a nose, an ear for an ear, a tooth for a tooth, and an equal wound for a wound. But whoever forgoes it in charity, it will serve as atone ment for him." Sure 5,45
	Palestine region
1.800 BC.	called "Canaan" in Mesopotamian texts and trade records

	Egyptian, Retune (Rtnw)
1.400 BC.	Hurru (Hùrú) pa-Hurru ([Land der] Hori[tes]), Erez Israel, Erez ha-Emori (Land der Amoriter), Erez Kena'an, Amoriter, Kanaan und Phönizien
722 BC.	Samerina instead of Samaria by the Assyrians "Erez Israel" ("Land of Israel") Erez ha-Ivrim („land of the Hebrews") "erez bene Israel" („land of the children of Israel")
500 BC.	"Palestine" in Herodotus' Histories Συρία ή Παλαιστίνη - Syria and Palestine, "the Philistine Syria" Persian province of Yehud with Jerusalem as its capital The land of Israel Jew (Yehudi)
500 BC.	τη Παλαιστίνη Συρίη – en de te Palaistine Syria (Herodotus) Φοίνικεςδε και Σύροι οι εν τη Παλαιστίνη - Phoinikes de kai syroi hoi en te palaistine
100 BC.	Judah (Yehud in Aramaic), the Greeks (Iouda, Ioudaia) and the Romans israel, land of: geographical survey (Judaea)
67 BC.	Judea when the Romans came "Palaistinei", biblical Canaan
136 AD.	Syria Palaestina, Philistaea, Roman Judea and Palestine, "Palaistinei" Finukyah (Phoenicia) and Aruvyah (Arabia)
300 AD.	"First", "Second" and "Third Palestine"
634 AD.	The Muslim armies rename "Syria Palestine" to "Jund Filastin" ("Military District of Palestine"). "Filastīn" for the "First Palestine"
1.096 AD.	by the European Christians as the "Holy Land"
1.948 AD.	State of Israel
9.000 BC.	**Jericho** (the oldest city in the world)
10.000	human settlements, from hunters and gatherers, nomadic life

3.3 million – 11.650	Paleolithic or Palaeolithic: Old Stone Age, development of stone tools
1.4 million	Some representatives of Homo erectus [Ur]
	most securely dated fossil site of the genus Homo outside Africa
600.000 – 8.000	Palaeolithic Age
600.000 BC.	Palaeolithic: Earliest human finds south of the Sea of Tabariyya (Tabaria, Sea of Galilee) [Musa]
250.000	Neanderthals (stone carving techniques attributed to them have been proven)
110.000	He can be traced back to Palestine 110,000 years ago
70.000	Hunters and fishermen: Big game hunting, including smaller animals and fishing, collecting activity
18.000	for more durable bearings, wild barley was ground and baked
12.000	Houses made of semi-circular stone settings with clay superstructures
11.000	Cereals were cultivated
10.000 – 2.000	Neolithic or New Stone Age: the introduction of farming, domestication of animals, and change from a hunter-gatherer lifestyle to one of settlement
9.500 – 8.800	Agriculture
8.000	Jericho: The town of perhaps 3000 people was surrounded by a wall 3 metres high
7700 – 7220 BC.	the town was uninhabited
8.000 – 5.000	Mesolithic: Sedentarisation, agriculture, domestic animal husbandry, lived in caves [Musa]
	Natufian culture: Mainly hunters, gathering wild grain at Ain Mallāha and Jericho
5.000 – 3.000	Chalcolithic: Copper and stone tools, the domestication of animals, the cultivation of crops, the production of pottery, the building of towns [br]
	Copper Age: At Beersheba there was a copper-working industry [br]
	En Gedi: a shrine of that period, and basketry, ivory, leather, and hundreds of copper ritual objects [br]

	the Ghassulians immigrated to Palestine [br]
3.300 – 1.200 BC	Bronze Age: Most of the towns, Megiddo, Jericho, Tall al-Farʿah, Tel Bet Sheʾan, Khirbat al-Karak, and Ai (Khirbat ʿAyy) in northern or central Palestine independent city-states
3.000 BC.	"Amorite-Canaanite wave" The Canaanites and the Phoenicians are one and the same Semitic people. [Musa]
4.000	International trade between the harbour city of Byblos and Egypt
2.000	Egypt's most important trading partner
3.100 – 2.00	Proto-Canaanite script, alphabetic script with 22 to 24 letters (Bronze Age)
2.000 – 1.500 BC.	Middle Bronze Age: new types of pottery, weapons, and burial practices, an urban civilization
	Tell el-Dab'a (Auaris): Palaces and temples, extensive burial grounds and a large number of residential buildings
2.000 – 1.550 BC.	Influence of the Hurrians, Syrians, horse-drawn chariots, military elite
1938 – 1756 BC.	Egyptian documents provide valuable information about Palestine, the Story of Sinuhe Bronze weapons at Megiddo, Jericho, and Tall al-ʿAjjul
1.550 BC.	the Egyptians' expulsion of the Hyksos into Palestine the destruction of Megiddo, Jericho, and Kiriath-sepher
	God
	Polytheism
	Belief in gods was an integral part of this area.
	El, Baal, Asherah, Elohim, Adonai, YHWH, Jesus Christ, Trinity, Allah, Mekal, the god, the lord of Beth Shean
	„Primus in orbe deos fecit timor" by Roman poet Publius Statius, "Fear made the first gods of the world" Existential fears, fears of survival, fear of hunger, fear of old age and helplessness The belief in gods of fertility was existential. The weather is chaotic and unpredictable. Earthquakes, drought, aridity, water shortages and crop failures were the great fears of mankind.

	In order to escape bitter chance and fate, people pray for blessing and mercy. Fertility was worshipped and idolised. God promises Abram offspring, fertile land and success [Genesis 12,1]. Who wouldn't go for it?
	Myths and fairy tales are often passed on orally as a form of entertainment.
El	
	from a root ʾyl or ʾwl, means "to be powerful", "power" The name "El" simply means "God"
	In Ugaritic Canaanite: as the personal name of the supreme god El, the head of the Canaanite pantheon, the ancestor of the other gods and goddesses, the creator of the earth and its creatures
	Ugarit (Ras Shamra): over 500 times in texts
	The Creator God and Father of Gods and Humans
	one of the oldest names for God in the Semitic language area
	Old, wise man depicted, sometimes with a beard
	El was the father of several important deities, including Baal
	Just like Zeus in Greek mythology
	Deity Dagon or Dagan: Northern Mesopotamia and Syria (e.g. from Ebla, Mari and Ugarit)
2.000	no evidence of YHWH worship
	"Isra-El", "El wins", god of war
1.600 BC.	Total population 140,000
Baal	
	"Prominent god who ruled over wind, clouds and rain, who could dry up harvests but also end droughts."
	Forces of nature and fertility, weather god
	in early Israel with the meaning "owner, master, lord"
	Storm god Hadad
1400 – 1200 BC.	Ugarit: detailed insights into the worship of Baal (main god) The storm god and god of rain and fertility

	Asherah
	a goddess of fertility
	El's wife
	Main deity, fertility, mother role and the earth (woman)
1400 – 1200 BC.	Ugarit: detailed information about Asherah
	spouse of the supreme god El
	"Mother of the gods" or "Mistress of the sea"
1.805 BC.	**Abraham**
	Legendary progenitor of the Semites (Jews and Arabs)
	born near the city of Ur in Mesopotamia (Irak, Amorite)
	The Canaanite King Melchisedek "King of Salem" already reigned in Jerusalem.
	From Ur to Palestine, a journey of over 2,000 kilometres, why from there?
	City of Ur - Babylonian captivity
	The text of Abraham was written down in the Babylonian captivity. The text shows the reference and the obligation to return home to Jerusalem and Palestine. That is why he had to return there. That was a Zionist ideology.
	Peoples of the Kaanites
	Phoenicians: as Phoenicians the Greek name and Canaanites or Canaanites the Hebrew name
4.00	Tulaylāt al-Ghassūl in the Jordan Valley: the Ghassulians immigrated to Palestine, the pottery and flints, copper axes were found in the south of Palestine
	the indigenous Neolithic-Chalcolithic population and the Ghassulians
	Neolithic-Chalcolithic population: 10.000 – 3.000 BC.
	Who were the ancient "Palestinian" Canaanites? The Semitic Amorites? Amorite: "They were troublesome nomads and were believed to be one of the causes of the downfall of the 3rd dynasty of Ur (c. 2112–c. 2004 BC)." [br] The Hurrians or the Hittites who came to Canaan from Anatolia?

	Hyksos: The Hyksos, a group of Asian peoples: dynasty of Palestinian origin that ruled northern Egypt as the 15th dynasty (c. 1630–c. 1530) by an influx of immigrants from Palestine into Egypt beginning about the 18th century BCE [br] Hyksos ruler of "the foreign lands" in Egypt
1.000 BC.	the Edomites in the south the Moabites east of the Dead Sea the Ammonites on the edge of the Syrian Desert east of Gilead [br]
2.000	**Hurrian and Hyksos rule**
	Hurrian armies undertook campaigns to Palestine and even to Egypt the horse-drawn chariots
	City of Hazor: the largest city in Canaan in the 15th to 13th centuries BC.
	Hurrian states are already known from the late 3rd millennium BC.
1.630 BC.	the Asiatic Hyksos: control of northern Egypt
1.648 – 1.550 BC.	The Great Hyksos Dynasty The Roman-Jewish historian Flavius Josephus described the Hyksos
1.550 – 1.150 BC.	**Egyptian rule**
Late Bronze Age	Gaza as a centre of power in the region
1.540 BC.	Pharao Kamose: He continued his fight against the Hyksos and was able to extend his sphere of influence to the north.
1.520 BC.	Pharao Ahmose I: He finally drove the Hyksos out of Egypt
1.479 – 1.426 BC.	Thutmosis III: There were campaigns to Palestine [Vee]
1.426 – 1.400 BC.	Amenophis II: There were campaigns to Palestine [Vee]
1.457 – 1.425 BC.	Thutmose III: Egyptian ruler, Thutmose the Great, was the sixth pharaoh of the 18th Dynasty

1.457 BC.	Battle of Megiddo: Thutmose III defeats a coalition of Syrian princes
	Military bases: Gaza, Jaffa, Beit She'an
	Large cities (over 10 ha): Gaza, Gath, Lakisz, Akko, Tyre, Hazor, Rehow, Szimon, Tel Mor, Tel Sera
	Ramses II - new military intervention in Palestine
1.400 – 1.390 BC.	Thutmosis IV: There were campaigns to Palestine [Vee]
1.390 – 1.353 BC.	Amenophis III: There were campaigns to Palestine [Vee]
1.360 BC.	Amenophis III: human group of the "Shasu-Yahu" (YHWH), in his temples in Soleb and Amara-West
1.319 – 1.292 BC.	Haremheb: There were campaigns to Palestine [Vee]
1.290 – 1.279 BC.	Sethos I: Raid in Palestine [Vee]
1.279 – 1.213 BC.	Ramses II: Raid in Palestine [Vee]
1.280 BC.	Stela ('First Stela') of Seti I (Northern Palestine): King Seti I, dominates Canaanite, group of rebellious Canaanite towns, Beth Shean, Hammath, Pella
	Seti I restored Egyptian authority in Canaan and rebuilt the Egyptian garrison at Beth Shean
	Stela ('Second Stela') of Seti I: the stability of trade routes in the Canaanite, a new road to Mesopotamia, east of the Anti-Lebanese mountains
1.261 BC.	Stela Ramesses II: generalised achievements of Ramesses II
	Mekal Stele (Canaanite): "Mekal, the god, the lord of Beth Shean", Mekal is seated on a throne
	Lion Stele (Canaanite): A Canaanite stele showing a lion and lioness at play was found in the excavation of the "governor's house".
1.274 BC.	Battle of Kadesh: wars between Egyptians and Hittites
	Financial contributions to Egypt increase
	Technical revolution: terracing and cisterns in the mountains, self-sufficiency, poverty, agriculture

1.276 BC.	Landing on the southern Mediterranean coast of Canaan Defeat during the invasion of Egypt by Ramses III. Mortuary temple of Ramses III: inscriptions and reliefs are said to show the Philistine army (Sea Peoples). Philistines and the Philistine country are documented in the Onomastikon des Amenope and the Inscription of Pediese.
	Circumcision: adopted by Egyptians, Phoenicians and the Syrians in Palestine
1.213 – 1.204 BC.	Merenptah: Raid in Palestine [Vee]
1.200 BC.	Total population 65,000, heterogeneous population, different cultures and traditions
1.200 BC.	hypothetical land grab However, there is no archaeological evidence of this land occupation.
1.208 BC.	Merenptah Stele: a victory stele with the name "**Israel**", Israel Stele, "Israel is devastated", Pharaoh Merenptah
	Israel - Connection with the god "El", "he fights against God", "God fights", "God proves to be ruler"
	Ephraim Promontory: Proto-Israelites on the hills, isolated on the mountains
1.187 – 1.156 BC.	Ramses III: Raid in Palestine [Vee]
1.155 BC.	Death of Pharaoh Ramses III
1.150 BC.	Collapse of the Egyptian empire
1.170 – 925 BC.	**Philistine rule**
1.185 BC.	Settlements along the coast, called Philistaea
	Migration: Sea peoples, foreign peoples, Crete, Aegean world, Greeks, Anatolia: Luka, Šardana, Danu, Peleset, Tjeker, Wašaš, ... one of the Sea Peoples, Peleset (Philistines), Palistin, coastal area between Gaza and Jaffy
	Enemies of Egypt, traces of devastation, city of Ugarit (1,188 BC)
	City states: Ashdod, Ashkelon, Ekron, Gat and Gaza (roughly south of today's Tel Aviv) excavation sites, i.e. in Ashdod, Tell el-Qasīle, Tēl Miqnē/Ekron and in Tell e-āfī/Gat,
	complicated and lengthy settlement process with the blessing and permission of Egypt

	Elite migration, ships, knowledge of sea routes, iron swords, pottery, weaving mills, rule cultural and political dominance, assimilation of the Semitic language and mixing with the natives Philistines: the hegemonic power in South Palestine
	excavation sites, i.e. in Ashdod, Tell el-Qasīle, Tēl Miqnē/Ekron and in Tell e-āfī/Gat
	Ashdod: the complete figure of the shape of a female chair (throne), Ashdoda, later gender reassignment Ashdoda bears witness to a direct connection to the Aegean figurines of seated women, worship of the great mother goddess Tell el-Qasīle: three superimposed temples, clay masks, cult stands, libation vessels, various small finds open libation vessel in the shape of a woman, connection to the Aegean cult of the Great Mother Goddess Ekron/Tēl Miqnē: hearth sanctuary, close links with Cyprus and the Aegean world, cult utensils, chalice (as in Cyprus), the wheels of a bronze cult stand (as in Cyprus) Temple complex from the 7th century, a complete dedicatory inscription with the name of the city of Ekron and the name of its ruler, which are known from the campaign of King Sanherib in 701 BC. The goddess of the temple: a goddess called Ptgjh (Pythogajah), a hybrid of the name of a sanctuary in Delphi, which was called "Pytho", with the name of the ancient Aegean mother goddess: Gaja. the worship of Baal in Ekron, a find of a female figure in Phoenician form, incense altars, feminine gods masculine god Baal, who has clear West Semitic roots Gat/Tell e-āfī: Two fragmentary lion-headed cups, bovine shoulder blades, libation vessels and a number of flower-shaped chalices Canaanite goddess Asherah, whose symbols included - alongside the lioness - a tree of life. fragmentary figurine of the El type Worship of the mother goddess, feminist traits
	Askalon: 19 clay jars apparently still in Crete and Cyprus Script: Cypro-Minoan as in Cyprus, Old Philistine script for their Indo-European language Similarities to the Minoan culture of the Mediterranean region (Crete, Cyprus)

	Close relations with the Egyptians (Mizrajim) 1.Moses 10,6-14
	"I brought Israel up from Egypt. I also brought the Philistines from Crete and the Arameans from Kir." Amos 9,7
	„Kaphtor", "Kaftor" - a term associated with the island of Crete.
	The genetic difference and the genetic distinguishing features are actually detectable for a short time.
	Through intermarriage, the gene pool has merged with the local population.
	They were rather a small people with nautical and military skills. They also mastered the art of building.
	They used iron for their iron weapons. They were good blacksmiths.
	They built an imposing building that could accommodate several hundred people.
	God of the Philistines: Dagon, Dagon was often depicted as a fish god or a grain god. A demon of the depths of the sea.
	Philistines: The home cult was the great mother goddess Kybele or Kybebe (Hittite Kubaba). The Bible associates the Philistines primarily with male deities, while archaeological findings tend to point to the predominance of the feminine.
1.000 BC.	Total population 170,000
925 BC.	**Palestine campaign**
	Sheshonq I: Palestine campaign, war of conquest and annihilation, hegemony of the Canaanite cities broken Gaza, Rafia, Arad, Gezer, Bet-Horon, Gibeon, Megiddo, Taanak, Bet-Szean are destroyed.
	Collapse: The political power of the Philistines is broken. Pharo withdraws to Egypt, leaving behind a political and military vacuum. The poor and insignificant highlanders (Israel) conquer the territory and plunder the cities of Canaan. The new state of Israel begins to take shape as organised crime through robbery, theft, robbery and looting.
	Dagon (God of the Philistines)
	Dagon: Heb. Dāgôn, male god Hebrew word dagh (fish), others with the Hebrew word da-ghán (grain), Semitic grain god

	West Semitic word for grain "dagan"	
	"hull", "Dagon's hull", "Dagon himself", "fish hull", "fish body", "fish part"	
	It was associated with fertility, harvest and agriculture (agrarian society)	
	"Then it turned east towards Beth Dagon. It touched Zebulun and the Valley of Iphtah El." Joshua 19,27	
1.300 BC.	Ugarit: a large temple to the deity Dagon Dagon is the father of Baal, Baal "son of Dagan"	
	Temples in Gaza (Samson, Judges 13-16, house with 2 pillars) and Ashdod	
	"he rulers of the Philistines gathered together. They were going to offer a great sacrifice to their god Dagon. They were going to celebrate. They said, 'Our god has handed our enemy Samson over to us." Judges 16,23	
	"Let me pay the Philistines back for what they did to my two eyes. Let me do it with only one blow." Judges 16,28	
	"Let me die together with the Philistines!' Then he pushed with all his might. The temple came down on the rulers." Judges 16,30	
	"They carried the ark into the temple of their god Dagon. They set it down beside the statue of Dagon." 1. Samuel 5,2	
	"There it was, lying on the ground again! It had fallen on its face in front of the ark of the LORD. Its head and hands had been broken off. Only the body of the statue was left. Its head and hands were lying in the doorway of the temple." 1. Samuel 5,4	
	"They said, 'The ark of the god of Israel must not stay here with us. His power is against us and against our god Dagon." 1. Samuel 5,7	
	The depictions in the Bible show a later depiction of a non-Israelite religion.	
	Rather during the time of the Maccabees, long after the Philistines were exterminated.	
	Mother Goddess (God of the Philistines)	
	Archaeology: predominantly female deities "Ashdoda" is the depiction of a seated woman whose body merges with her chair.	
	The prevalence of the feminine in the cult of the Philistines: the jars at Tell el-Qasil and the 7th-century dedicatory inscription from Ekron.	
	multi-cultural philistine world	
	In the earliest stages of their colonisation	

Time and place unknown	**Taking of Canaan** (Bible)
	"I will give all of you every place you walk on, just as I promised Moses." Joshua 1,3

"Your territory will reach from the Negev Desert all the way to Lebanon. The great River Euphrates will be to the east. The Mediterranean Sea will be to the west. Your territory will include all the Hittite country." Joshua 1,4

"Be strong and brave. You will lead these people. They will take the land as their very own. It is the land I promised to give their people of long ago." Joshua 1,6

"'We're sure the LORD has given the whole land over to us. All the people there are weak with fear because of us." Joshua 2,24 |
| | "You will soon know that the living God is among you. He will certainly drive out the people now living in the land. He'll do it to make room for you. He'll drive out the Canaanites, Hittites, Hivites, Perizzites, Girgashites, Amorites and Jebusites." Joshua 3,10 |
| | "So Joshua brought the whole area under his control. That included the central hill country and the Negev Desert. It included the western hills and the mountain slopes. It also included all the kings in that whole area. Joshua didn't leave anyone alive. He totally destroyed everyone who breathed. He did just as the LORD, the God of Israel, had commanded. Joshua brought everyone from Kadesh Barnea to Gaza under his control. He did the same thing to everyone from the whole area of Goshen to Gibeon. He won the battle over all those kings and their lands. He did it in one campaign. That's because the LORD, the God of Israel, fought for Israel." Joshua 10,40-42

"The LORD handed them over to Israel. The Israelites won the battle over them. They hunted them down all the way to Greater Sidon. They chased them to Misrephoth Maim. They chased them to the Valley of Mizpah in the east. Not one of them was left alive." Joshua 11,8 |
| | "So Joshua captured the whole land. He took over the central hill country and the whole Negev Desert. He took over the whole area of Goshen. He took over the western hills. He took over the Arabah Valley. He took over the mountains of Israel and the hills around them. He took over the area that begins at Mount Halak, which rises towards Seir. The area ends at Baal Gad in the Valley of Lebanon below Mount Hermon. Joshua captured the kings who ruled over that whole land. He put them to death."

Joshua 11,16-17 |

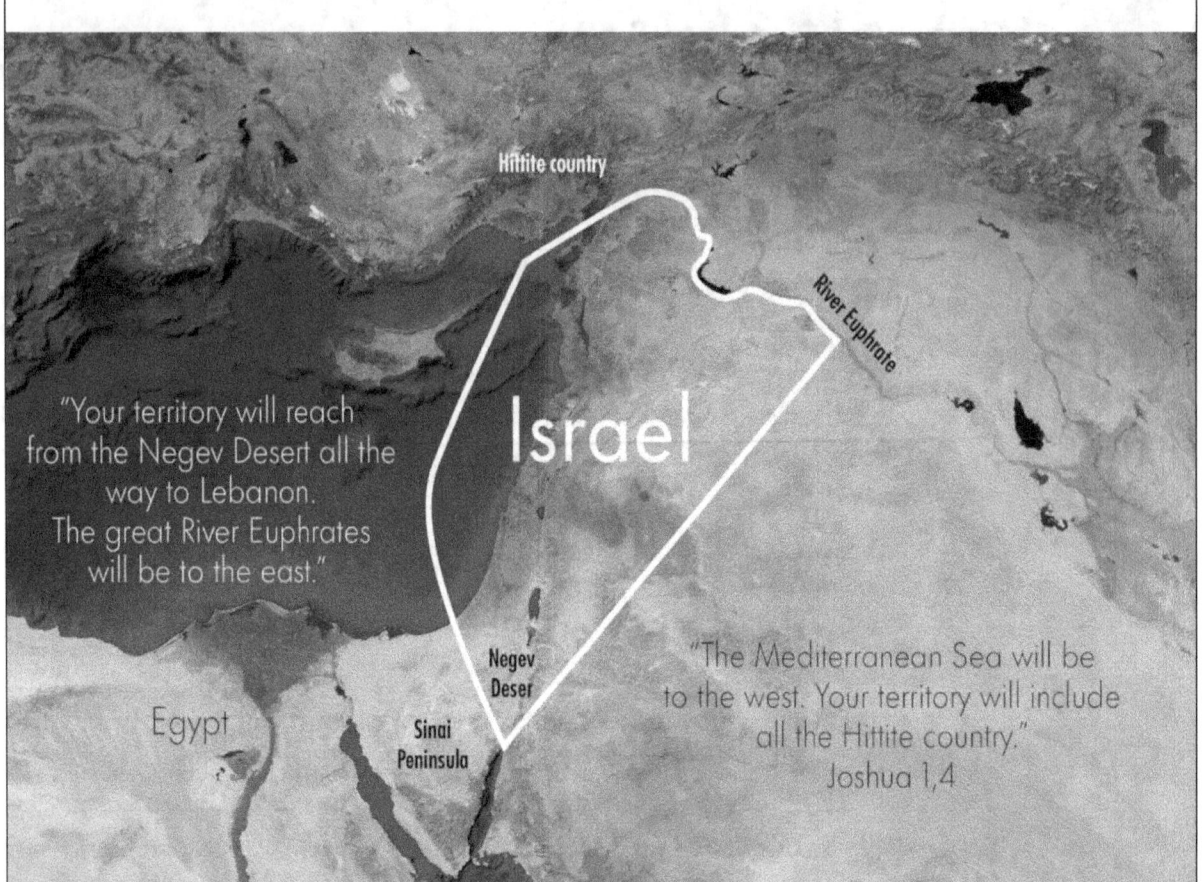

"Your territory will reach from the Negev Desert all the way to Lebanon. The great River Euphrates will be to the east."

Israel

River Euphrate

"The Mediterranean Sea will be to the west. Your territory will include all the Hittite country."
Joshua 1,4

Hittite country

Negev Deser

Egypt

Sinai Peninsula

God's vision for Israel by Joshua

Abraham's heritage

„The Israelites took over the territory east of the River Jordan.

The land they captured reached from the River Arnon valley to Mount Hermon. It included the whole east side of the Arabah Valley. Israel won the battle over the kings of that whole territory. Here are the lands Israel captured from the kings they won the battle over.

They took over the land of Sihon. He was the king of the Amorites. He ruled in Heshbon. The land he ruled over begins at Aroer. Aroer is on the rim of the River Arnon valley. Sihon ruled from the middle of the valley to the River Jabbok. The Jabbok is the border of Ammon. Sihon's territory included half of Gilead.

He also ruled over the east side of the Arabah Valley. That land begins at the Sea of Galilee. It goes to the Dead Sea and over to Beth Jeshimoth. Then it goes south, below the slopes of Pisgah. Israel also took over the territory of Og. He was the king of Bashan. He was one of the last of the Rephaites. He ruled in Ashtaroth and Edrei.

He ruled over Mount Hermon, Salekah and the whole land of Bashan. Og's kingdom reached all the way to the border of Geshur and Maakah. He ruled over half of Gilead. His land reached the border of Sihon, the king of Heshbon. Moses was the servant of the LORD. Moses and the Israelites won the battle over those two kings. He gave their land to the tribes of Reuben and Gad and half of the tribe of Manasseh. He gave it to them as their share. Joshua and the Israelites won the battle over the kings who ruled west of the River Jordan. The lands of those kings reached from Baal Gad in the Valley of Lebanon to Mount Halak, which rises towards Seir. Joshua gave their lands to the tribes of Israel as their very own. He divided them up and gave each tribe its share. Those lands included the central hill country, the western hills and the Arabah Valley. They also included the mountain slopes, the Desert of Judah and the Negev Desert. Those lands belonged to the Hittites, Amorites, Canaanites, Perizzites, Hivites and Jebusites.

Here are the kings Israel won the battle over.

The king of Jericho one, the king of Ai, which is near Bethel one, the king of Jerusalem one, the king of Hebron one, the king of Jarmuth one, the king of Lachish one, the king of Eglon one, the king of Gezer one, the king of Debir one, the king of Geder one, the king of Hormah one, the king of Arad one, the king of Libnah one, the king of Adullam one, the king of Makkedah one, the king of Bethel one, the king of Tappuah one, the king of Hepher one, the king of Aphek one, the king of Lasharon one, the king of Madon one, the king of Hazor one, the king of Shimron Meron one, the king of Akshaph one, the king of Taanach one, the king of Megiddo one, the king of Kedesh one, the king of Jokneam in Carmel one, the king of Dor in Naphoth Dor one, the king of Goyim in Gilgal one, the king of Tirzah one,

The total number of kings was 31." Joshua 12,1-24

Time and place unknown	**Permanent wars** (Bible)
	"Abraham stayed in the land of the Philistines for a long time." Genesis 21:34
	"He was working out his plans against the Philistines. That's because the Philistines were ruling over Israel at that time." Judges 14,4
	"The ark of the LORD had been in Philistine territory for seven months." 1. Samuel 6,1
	"That day the Israelites struck down the Philistines. They killed them from Mikmash to Aijalon. By that time they were tired and worn out." 1. Samuel 14,31
	"So David won the fight against Goliath with a sling and a stone. He struck down the Philistine and killed him. He did it without even using a sword." 1. Samuel 17,50
	"So he asked the LORD for advice. He said, 'Should I go and attack those Philistines?' The LORD answered him, 'Go and attack them. Save Keilah.'" 1. Samuel 23,2

"Just then a messenger came to Saul. He said, 'Come quickly! The Philistines are attacking the land.'" 1. Samuel 23,27

"So David asked the LORD for advice. He said, 'Should I go and attack the Philistines? Will you hand them over to me?' The LORD answered him, 'Go. I will surely hand over the Philistines to you.'" 2. Samuel 5,19

"For he wiped out his enemies on every side and scorned his adversaries the Philistines; he crushed their power to our own day." Jesus Sirach 47,7

"he subdued the leaders of the enemy and all the rulers of the Philistines." Jesus Sirach 46,18

"a mongrel people shall settle in Ashdod, and I will make an end of the pride of Philistia." Zechariah 9,6

„Two nations my soul detests, and the third is not even a nation:
those who live in Seir and the Philistines and the foolish people who live in Shechem."
Jesus Sirach 50,25-26

"Woe, inhabitants of the seacoast, you nation of the Cherethites! The word of the Lord is against you, O Canaan, land of the Philistines, and I will destroy you until no inhabitant is left." Zefanja 2,5

"While David was king of Israel, he won many battles over the Philistines. He brought them under his control. He took Gath away from the Philistines. He also captured the villages around Gath." 1 Chronicles 18:1

"So David did just as God had commanded him. He and his men struck down the Philistine army. They struck them down from Gibeon all the way to Gezer." 1. Chronicles 14,16

"A mighty hero named Goliath came out of the Philistine camp. He was from Gath. He was more than 3.25 metres tall."

1.Samuel 17,4

"They put Saul's armour in the temple where they had set up statues of female gods that were named Ashtoreth. They hung his body up on the wall of Beth Shan." 1.Samuel 31,10

Battle of Eben-Eser: The Philistines capture the Ark of the Covenant and set it up in the temple of their god Dagan in Ashdod. 1.Samuel 4

Battle of Mount Gilboa: The Philistines behead Israel's king Saul and his sons, then drape the bodies on the city wall of Beth Shean (the goddess Ashtoret or Astarte). 1.Samuel 31

The Ark of the Covenant in the Temple of Dagon: Dagon's statue topples over, head and hands break off, the body lies there alone. 1.Samuel 5
The Israelites were mocking the god Dogan and the Philistines.

Three Hated Nations	
	"There are two nations that I detest, and a third that does not even deserve to be called a nation. These are the Edomites, the inhabitants of the Philistine cities, and the stupid Samaritans." Sirach 50:25-27
El (Bible)	
	El Shaddai (אל שדי): Often translated as "God the Almighty", "Almighty", "Omnipotent", "sufficient, capable", "God of the mountains" El Schaddai, is only used in connection with Abraham, Isaac and Jacob in Genesis.
	El Elyon (אל עליון): Means "God, the Highest", "higher, above", "highest", "Most High", "the Most High" "Melchizedek was the king of Jerusalem", „He was the priest of the Most High God [ʾEl ʿElyon]", "He gave a blessing to Abram." " May the Creator of heaven and earth bless him." Genesis 14:18 "While among the pagans the term referred to the God who was superior to the other gods, in Israel the term referred to the transcendent beings of the one true God."
	El Olam (אל עולם): Means "God of eternity" or "eternal God", "the eternal God", "the God of an infinitely long time", "the creator of the ends of the earth"
	El Roi (אל ראי): Means "God who sees me", "the God of vision", "the God who sees me"
	El Bethel (אל בית־אל): Means "God of Bethel"
	El Gibbor (אל גבור): Means "mighty God" or "strong God"
	El Berit (אל ברית): "God of the covenant", as the divine protector of the covenants
	ELOAH, Elohim(אלוהים): The word ʾeloah "God" and its plural, elohim, is apparently a lengthened form of El The plural form elohim is used for pagan "gods", but also for a single pagan "god" and even for a "goddess". He is mentioned 2,000 times as the God of Israel, haʾelohim, "the [true] God" "the deity" "The word elohim is also used to describe someone or something as godlike, supernatural or exceptionally great."
	Isra-El: "who fights with God" or "God-fighter", Genesis 32,29

	Ismael: "God hears", Genesis 16,11
	Bet-El: "House of God"
	Penu-El: "God's face", Genesis 32,31
	"God of Abraham" (El Avraham)
	"God of Isaac" (El Jitzchaq)
	"God of Jacob" (El Ja'aqov)
	Samuel, Joel, Gabriel or Immanuel, with the theophoric element "El"
YHWH-Jahweh	
	hebraic: יהוה, often transliterated as "YHWH from the root hwh, which is an older variant of the root hyh "to be" "He causes that which is, he brings into being." "I-am-who-I-am" (a folk etymology) God of the desert
	From Old North Arabic, from the weather god of the Baal-Hadad type (J. Wellhausen): "The name Yahweh seems to mean: he travels through the air, he blows"
	originally a weather god of the nomads in today's southern Jordan
1.360 BC.	Inscriptions of Pharaoh Amenophis III, a group of nomads known as the "Shasu of YHW".
	Origin in the region of Midian (today's north-west Saudi Arabia), Moses' connection to Midian (Exodus 3:1-15)?
860 BC.	Mesha Stele: "Omri, the king of **Israel**" and a few lines later "the altars of **YHWH**"
800 BC.	Inscriptions from Kuntillet Ajrud and Khirbet el-Qom: "**Yahweh** and his **Asherah**"
	Asherah as consort or divine partner of Yahweh
	Asherah poles or "Asherim", an Asherah figure
760 BC.	Kuntillet Adschrud: 200 kg stone bowl in the short form jhw, jhwh in an inscription on wall plaster, as the ending -jw in various personal names, and as jhwh in letter forms on storage jars (-jw in Israel) "**YHWH** of Samaria" and "**YHWH** of Teman"
	"Creator of heaven and earth" (Genesis 14,19), "the Creator of Israel" (Isaiah 43,15), "the Holy One", "the Holy One of Israel", "the Shepherd of Israel", "King of Israel"
David	

	No king, bandit, warlord, robber, clan leader, gang of daredevils, gangsters and rogues, warrior, murderer
	Force of 400 to 600 fighters
	Tel Dan inscription, "House of David" inscription, the existence of a "Dynasty of David" in the 9th/8th century BC.
	no proof of a united kingdom of Israel and Judah under the biblical King David
	Solomon
	The myth of Solomon, a legendary, fictitious figure, for which there is a lack of evidence and indications of historicity "After all, there is no other evidence for him apart from the Bible.", Rostock theologian Hermann Michael Niemann
	the Proverbs of Solomon, the Preacher Solomon, the Song of Solomon (Song of Songs) - 4th century BC at the earliest.
	Around 1,000 BC, there was no significant written culture in Israel.
926 – 734 BC.	**Kingdom of Israel**
	"Samuel wasn't pleased when they said, 'Give us a king to lead us.' So he prayed to the LORD." 1. Samuel 8,6
	"In spite of what Samuel said, the people refused to listen to him. 'No!' they said. 'We want a king to rule over us. Then we'll be like all the other nations. We'll have a king to lead us. He'll go out at the head of our armies and fight our battles.'" 1. Samuel 8,19-20
926 – 882 BC.	Pre-royal Israel: Jeroboam (thanks to Sheshonq I), Nadab, Baazza, Zimri - In the foothills of the Ephraim Mountains Short reigns, coups d'état, military overthrows, simple living conditions, no palace, small city
882 – 723 BC.	Kingdom of Israel: Tibni, **Omri** (1st king), Ahab, Ahaziah, Joram, Jehu, Joahas, Joash, Jeroboam II., Zechariah, ..., Hoshea State, residential city of Samaria, walled royal palace, civil service, army, taxes, temple and priests
882 – 871	**1st King Omri**
	The dynasty of rulers founded by Omri is known as the Omri dynasty: Ahab, Ahaziah, Joram, Jehu

	Ahasja: 'YHWH has taken hold' Joram: 'YHWH is exalted' Jehu: 'YHWH is he' Joahas: 'JHWH has taken hold' Joash: 'YHWH has given a gift' Zechariah: 'YHWH has remembered' Menahem: 'YHWH has comforted' Pekachya: 'YHWH is open'	
	He bought Mount Samaria and built a city on the mountain and called it Samaria. 1. Kings 16,24	
	Achab: the son of Omri, king over Israel and reigned over Israel in Samaria.	
	and erected an altar to Baal, And Ahab made an Asherah	
	The Mesha Stele: the Moabite king Mesha praises the liberation of his people from dependence and tribute to the northern kingdom of Israel. The name **YHWH** is also mentioned there. The "King of **Israel**" was his opponent. "Omri the king of Israel oppressed" Moab "many days"	
841 BC.	so-called Black Obelisk: Assyrian king Salmanasser III, in Nimrud, Jehu stands as "son of Omri"	
	This is the beginning of the worship of YHWH and only through the Omrids, the dynasty of the Omrids The god YHWH is a dynastic god.	
853 BC.	Battle of Karkar: Israel has 2,000 chariots, the most of any ally, military strength, hegemony	
	Growth: robbery, plundering, theft, appropriation, forced labour, indentured servitude, exploitation of the conquered population	
845 – 586 BC.	**Kingdom of Judah**	
845 – 697 BC.	Kingdom of Judah: Atalya, Joash, Amaziah, Azariah, Jotham, Achaz, Ezechias Formed and moulded by the rule of Israel, later develops his own identity as king	
	Joash: 'YHWH has given a gift' Amazja: 'Strong is YHWH' Jotam: 'YHWH is perfect'	

	Jojakim: 'the Lord will raise up'
	Jojachin: 'the Lord confirms'
	Zedekiah: 'YHWH is (my) righteousness'
850 BC.	Northern Kingdom (Israel) with the capital Samaria and Southern Kingdom (Judah) with the capital Jerusalem
	constant disputes, conflicts, competition, subjugation and power struggles between these realms
841 – 820 BC.	The Aramean king Hazael defeated the Philistines, among others, and conquered the great Gath.
787 BC.	Israel: power struggles for the throne, several coups, coup d'état, crisis of the royal monarchy
	For southern Palestine, Judah and Jerusalem, on the other hand, there is no evidence of the belief in YHWH until the 8th century BC.
	He was the national god at the beginning of the 7th century BC.
	Inscription from Khirbet Bet Ley: "YHWH the God of the whole land, the mountains of Judah to the God of Jerusalem."
734 – 630 BC.	**Assyrian rule**
734 BC.	Tiglath-Pileser III: The Assyrians conquer Gaza and other Philistine coastal towns, resettlement, expulsion (13,250 people from Israel)
	Israel and Judah are subjugated. They have to pay tribute.
722 BC.	Foundation of Samerina, conquest of Samaria by the Assyrians, destruction of the palace, deportation (27,290 people)
	ten tribes go into exile - the Ten Lost Tribes, the Judean Shefela Plain is massively depopulated
720 BC.	Uprising and rebellion in Gaza and other philistine cities
	Apparently, the Philistine society then split into a pro-Assyrian and an anti-Assyrian party.
	Five large cities of the Philistines, the Philistine cities of Ashdod and Gath, were subject to tribute.

701 BC.	Sennacherib's 3rd campaign against the Jewish king Hezekiah: I took 46 of its strong, fortified cities and the countless towns around them, plundered them and regarded them as spoils of war
	Deportation of members of the royal family, parts of the population and livestock to Assyria. As booty, 30 talents of gold and 300 talents of silver were taken from Jerusalem. Judah as a vassal state
	The Kingdom of Judah only existed in its heartland (the Jerusalem region).
700 BC.	Total population 400,000
700 – 630 BC.	Pax Assyriaca Jerusalem grows to 60 hectares, the wall is heavily fortified, military expenditure on the city wall
	Some Philistine cities experienced an economic boom. Ekron grew from 4 to a good 34 hectares, and new settlements with a total settlement area of just under 27 hectares were built around Gat. In the Gaza region, the two 10-hectare towns of Tell er-Ruqeish and Blakhijeh have been rebuilt. Ekron - centre of olive oil production and the textile industry The area of the olive oil industry seems to have extended as far as Tell Hadid, for example. Ashkelon - centre of wine production Many smaller towns in the area were connected to the industry.
	Philistines, Canaanites, Assyrians, Egyptians, Greeks and Judeans now bustled about in the large cities.
716 – 586 BC.	Judah: Ezechiasz, Manasses, Amon, Jozjasz, Jehojakim, Jehojakin, Sedecjasz, Gedaliasz - stable development
640 – 604 BC.	**Egyptian dominance**
	Egypt again strongest and dominant power, small expansion of Judah, henotheism of Yahweh
605 – 539 BC.	**Babylonian rule**
605 BC.	Battle of Karkemiš: Babylon defeats the Egyptian army

604 BC.	Ashkelon was "turned into a heap of ruins" and the king of Ashkelon was led into exile. Ekron seems destroyed
600 BC.	Conquest of Ashdod: The Philistines were wiped out by Nebuchadnezzar. After that, their name no longer appears. The Philistine people were wiped out and ceased to exist. Disappearance of the Philistines at the end of the 7th century.
586 BC.	the Neo-Babylonian king **Nebuchadnezzar II**: Destruction of Jerusalem and the Temple, scorched earth tactics
586 – 538 BC.	**Babylonian captivity, Babylonian exile**, Deportation (597 and 586), 85% of the settlements destroyed Circumcision and pasha as identity creators, elite creates religious Yahweh revolution
538 – 302 BC.	**Persian rule**
	Persian province of Yehud with Jerusalem as its capital, Jerusalem ruled by a priestly elite, 20th - 30,000 inhabitants (330 BC.) Gaza: Granary for the Persian army
	Synagogues are established in the Diaspora and the Jewish faith is now proclaimed through the word of God.
539 BC.	Cyrus II of Persia: Conquest of Babylon by the Persian king Cyrus the Great
	Cyrosus cylinder, first writing of the "human rights", liberal and tolerant, Aramaic - language of the Persians
539 – 424 BC.	Waves of Jews returning to Jerusalem (539 - 529, 521 - 515, 465 - 424 BC.), organised by the royal elite of Judah.
	Yahweh: the polytheism finally eradicated, monotheism
	Jewish priests collect and write down Jewish stories systematically for the first time. "The scribes fudge history", they concealed their political and religious ideas in the stories. The main goal: the theocracy of God in the free state of Israel The true authors and the time of recording are deliberately concealed. The word of God was manipulated in this way.

	You even invent biblical protagonists and present yourself as idealistic, unnatural and great in your own inferiority complex. Like Moses, Joseph, David, Solomon, Abraham, Joshua, Daniel, Egyptian plagues and victorious wars, …
	Of course, the authors had hardly any historical documents or information from this period at their disposal.
	The Internet and Google were not invented. There were no databases with billions of pieces of information.
	Who can say what someone did 1,000 years ago? How would you really know the ancestry lists and names?
	The commandment of circumcision, the ban on marrying a foreign woman, could only have originated in Mesopotamia.
	Because circumcision was completely normal in Egypt. But not in Babylon. Even in captivity, it was important to preserve one's own Jewish identity. A mixed marriage would be fatal.
	The Jewish religious texts were imported from Babylon to Jerusalem and enforced there.
	The Jewish religion is exclusive to Jews. Non-Jews have no access and are not welcome. The inner temple area in Jerusalem was taboo for non-Jews and punishable by death.
	The God YHWH, the Creator of the universe, belongs only to them. In principle, this is a contradiction in terms.
515 BC.	the temple was rebuilt
	Judah never again had a king, no more royal rule
	Priests become elite and rulers in Judah and Jerusalem, they are tax collectors, judges and land administrators
	New theology: transcendence of God, paradise, perfection of God, purity law, dietary regulations, order of God
486 – 466 BC.	Xerxes I. a Persian great king
	Tension between "chosen people" (exodus experience in Babylonia) and "people of the earth" (no deportation)
330 – 63 BC.	**Hellenistic rule**
332 BC.	Gaza and Tyre defeated

	Alexander the Great: Hellenistic culture, enlistment of Jewish men in his army, high priest in Jerusalem
	The rule of the Ptolemies in Egypt, Alexandria as the centre of power
	the Hellenistic exile and the Hellenistic diaspora, Alexandria, Hebrew-Aramaic Bible into Greek, Septuagint LXX
250 – 100	Septuagint LXX
201 BC.	The Seleucid Antiochus (Seleucid Empire) occupies large parts of Palestine
168 BC.	The Jewish religion is abolished by the Seleucid Antiochos IV Epiphanes.
167 BC.	The temple of Jerusalem is plundered. Jerusalem was to be Hellenised.
166 – 160 BC.	Uprising and rebellion of the Maccabees (Hasmoneans), civil war, power struggle in Jerusalem, territorial expansion
142 – 129 BC.	Jewish autonomy under the Hasmoneans, from high priest to king: religion, politics and military in one hand
129 – 63 BC.	**Hasmonean monarchy**
	Jewish independence under the Hasmonean monarchy, forced conversion and conversion to Judaism, circumcision
	Idea: Unity through religious affiliation to Yahweh and God's law (Torah), Jerusalem as the only place of worship
	The last independent kingdom of Judea
	The Judean Maccabees wage war against the Philistines, destroy Javneh and conquer Gezer.
	Israel: from Dan to Beer-Szeby, the greatest expansion and conquest of the Jews, as great as that of David and Solomon
	Intensive editing and rewriting of Hebrew scriptures such as "Books of the Maccabees", "Song of Songs", Genesis
	Ashdod: A temple of Dagon was devastated by Jonathan.
	"When he approached Azotus, they showed him the burnt-out temple of Dagon, and Azotus and its suburbs destroyed, and the corpses lying about, and the charred bodies of those whom Jonathan[c] had burned in the war, for they had piled them in heaps along his route." 1. Maccabees 11,4

63 BC. – 337 AD.	**Roman rule**
	Conquest by the Roman general Pompey, Roman rule
27 BC. – 192 AD.	Pax Romana or Pax Augusta
20 BC. – 63 AD.	Complex reconstruction of the sanctuary on the Temple Mount, the builder Herod shines like the new mythical King Solomon
	Romans desecrate the temple of the Jews, erect statues of Jupiter, even help themselves to the temple treasury
	Christianity
	Beginning of faith in Jesus Christ, the Messiah of the world
	Trinity of Father, Son and Spirit
	Jesus Christ - man and God at the same time
	good news, the gospel, „Metanoeite!" – Turn your mind around! Think about it!
	"Love the Lord your God with all your heart and with all your soul. Love him with all your mind and with all your strength."
	And here is the second one. "Love your neighbour as you love yourself." There is no commandment more important than these.' Mark 12,30-31
	cosmopolitan
30 AD.	**New Testament**
	"Above his head they placed the written charge against him. It read, This is Jesus, the King of the Jews." Matthew 27,37
	"Then they fell on their knees in front of him and made fun of him. 'We honour you, king of the Jews!'" Matthew 27,29
	"They began to call out to him, 'We honour you, king of the Jews!'" Mark 15,18
	"They said, 'If you are the king of the Jews, save yourself.'" Luke 23,37
	"Salvation comes from the Jews." John 4,22
	"Jesus was doing these things on the Sabbath day. So the Jewish leaders began to oppose him." John 5,16
	"After this, Jesus went around in Galilee. He didn't want to travel around in Judea. That was because the Jewish leaders there were looking for a way to kill him." John 7,1

	"They kept saying, 'We honour you, king of the Jews!' And they slapped him in the face." John 19,3
	"The chief priests of the Jews argued with Pilate. They said, 'Do not write "The King of the Jews." Write that this man claimed to be king of the Jews.'" John 19,21
	"It is God's power to save everyone who believes. It is meant first for the Jews. It is meant also for the Gentiles." Romans 1,16
	"Or is God the God of Jews only? Isn't he also the God of Gentiles? Yes, he is their God too." Romans 3,29
	"Jews require signs. Greeks look for wisdom." 1. Corinthians 1,22
	"We are Jews by birth. We are not sinful Gentiles." Galatians 2,15
	"I know that you suffer and are poor. But you are rich! Some people say they are Jews but are not. I know that their words are evil. Their worship comes from Satan." Revelation 2,9
	"Let this Messiah, this king of Israel, come down now from the cross! When we see that, we will believe.' Those who were being crucified with Jesus also made fun of him." Mark 15,32
	"It is not as though the word of God has failed. For not all those descended from Israel are Israelites" Romans 9,6
New era	
38 AD.	The world's first pogrom: Greeks against Jews in Alexandria, murder, arson, Ghetto - the first ghetto in the world
66 AD.	Rebellion and uprising against the Romans, conquest of the Masada fortress, murder of Roman servants and soldiers
66 – 70 AD.	Great Jewish War (1st War of Liberation), conquest of Jerusalem, destruction and burning of the Temple
70 – 135 AD.	Complete control by the Romans, Diaspora uprising (2nd liberation struggle) and Bar Kochba uprising (3rd liberation struggle)
115 – 117 AD.	Diaspora uprising (2nd liberation struggle): End of the diaspora in Alexandria, Cyrenaica, Egypt, Cyprus and Mesopotamia
135 AD.	Bar-Kochba (3rd liberation struggle): Judea renamed Syria Palestine, capital remains Jerusalem, Roman colony

	Entry and residence ban for Jews in Jerusalem and the surrounding area (Emperor Hadrian), sale of Jews as slaves
	Urbanization through Hellenistic and Roman influences, colourful mixture of religions and gods
	The Judeans had more than 500,000 (?) fighters killed!
	Syria Palestine: after the two traditional enemies of the Jews, the Syrians and the Philistines
	City of Aelia Capitolina, built on the ruins of Jerusalem
	Anthedon and Gaza: 90 ha each, Ashkelon: 52 ha, Javne: 50 ha, Azotus Paralius: 40 ha, Gaza-Maiumas: 30 ha, Antipatris and Rafah: 12 ha, Ashdod and Jaffa shrank to 10 and 4 ha respectively
	Jewish diaspora: No Zionist ideology, no longing for Palestine, Yahweh cult in the synagogues Diaspora as a blessing and not a punishment from God
312 AD.	Emperor Constantine: Battle of the Milvian Bridge, conversion to Christianity, first Christian on the Roman imperial throne
325 AD.	The Confession of Nicaea: the Trinitarian formulation of the confession as God the Father, God the Son and God the Spirit
337 – 640 AD.	**Byzantine rule**
	Processes of demarcation between Christianity and Judaism, anti-Judaism, Sabbath, holidays, rituals
	Some cities are losing their urban character and society as a whole is becoming more rural.
370 AD.	Jerusalem Talmud, Palestinian Talmud, Palestinian Talmud: teaching and study, practical book for rabbis the Jewish code of conduct Talmud: 248 commandments and 365 prohibitions
395 AD.	Partition: Roman Empire with Rome and Eastern Roman Empire with Byzantium (Constantinople)
500 AD.	90% Christians, 10% Jews in Palestine and Samaritans, churches everywhere, monastery, Patriarchate of Jerusalem, Church of Jerusalem 118 synagogues, churches and synagogues side by side in Gaza
529 AD.	Jewish pogrom against Christians: Destruction of churches, murder, burning down of houses, murder of priests

600 AD.	The Babylonian Talmud, encyclopedia, lots of information for Jewish teaching
	Islam
600 AD.	Origin of Islam in today's Saudi Arabia, roots in Judaism and Christianity, Abraham, Ishmael, Hagar, Jesus, Mary
	many borrowings from the Old and New Testaments In the Koran, Jesus is a highly esteemed prophet like Abraham, Moses and Noah. But not as God. Within 20 years, the archangel Gabriel dictated the verses of the Koran to Mohammed.
	Earthquakes and natural disasters have struck the Middle East and made people more open to new solutions, new help, new religion.
	Koran
	The major world religions such as Judaism, Christianity and Islam compete with each other and do not accept each other. Each believes itself to be in possession of the pure truth. Islam clearly distances itself from the Torah and the Bible and speaks of the only true faith in Allah. The other two religions have gone astray and are false beliefs. This is not a basis for cooperation and is the cause of enmity. Islam rejects Judaism and Christianity.
	"O you who believe! Do not take the Jews and the Christians as allies (auliyā)." Sure 5, 51 auliyā – "Friends", "helpers", "supporters", "protectors", "confidants", "patrons", "leaders" "Christians have transgressed boundaries by idolizing a mortal." Ahmad S. 847 "False doctrine of sonship with God." Ahmad S. 847 "Trinity doctrine is unacceptable." Ahmad S. 847 "Doctrine of atonement is wrong." Ahmad S. 847
	"The Jews said, "Ezra is the son of God," and the Christians said, "The Messiah is the son of God." May God assail them! How deceived they are!" Sure 9,30
	"The Messiah son of Mary was only a Messenger, before whom other Messengers had passed away, and his mother was a woman of truth." Sure 5,75

	"But as for those who disbelieve and deny Our signs—these are the inmates of the Fire." Sure 5,86
	"Those who believe, and those who are Jewish, and the Sabeans, and the Chris tians, and the Zoroastrians, and the Poly theists—God will judge between them on the Day of Resurrection. God is witness to all things." Sure 22,17
	"Had the People of the Book (Torah and Bible) believed and been righteous, We would have remit ted their sins, and admitted them into the Gardens of Bliss.." Sure 5,65
	„ Say, "O People of the Scripture, you have no basis until you uphold the Torah, and the Gospel, and what is revealed to you from your Lord." … your Lord will increase many of them in rebellion and disbelief, so do not be sorry for the disbelieving people. " Sure 5,68
	"Those who believe, and those who are Jewish, and the Christians, and the Sabeans— any who believe in God and the Last Day, and act righteously—will have their reward with their Lord—they have nothing to fear, nor will they grieve." Sure 2,62
	"The Jews say, "The Christians are not based on anything," and the Christians say, "The Jews are not based on anything." Yet they both read the Scripture." Sure 2,113
	"Say, "God's (Allah) guidance is the guid ance." Sure 2,120
	"And they say, "Be Jews or Christians, and you will be guided." Say, "Rather, the religion of Abraham, the monotheist; he was not an idolater."" Sure 2,135
	"And from those who say, "We are Christians," We received their pledge, but they neglected some of what they were reminded of. So We provoked enmity and hatred among them until the Day of Resurrection; God will then inform them of what they used to craft." Sure 5,14
	"The Jews and the Christians say, "We are the children of God, and His beloved." Say, "Why then does He punish you for your sins?" In fact, you are humans from among those He created." Sure 5,18
	"Had the People of the Scripture believed, it would have been better for them. Among them are the believers, but most of them are sinners." Sure 3,110
622 AD.	The Islamic calendar begins with the so-called 'Hijrah', the migration of Muhammad from Mecca to Medina
	Allah
	The word "Allah" is the Arabic word for God (El), as God El is for Jews
	The word is derived from the Aramaic "Alaha" and the Hebrew "Elohim".
	He is omniscient, omnipotent, omnipresent.

	For Jews and Christians, their God has the same characteristics.
	Jerusalem
	The same place is sacred to the three world religions: Jerusalem.

Temple of Yahweh: destroyed by the Romans in 70 AD.

Golgotha: Christ was crucified in Jerusalem and often visited the temple himself. He preached here for some time.

Temple Mount: The rapture of Muhammad from Mecca to Jerusalem and his ascension from the rock on the Temple Mount. The Dome of the Rock is there. |
| 614 AD. | **Persian invasion** |
| | Conquest of Jerusalem, flight of Christians to Jordan, Alexandria, Africa, Constantinople

Sacking of Jerusalem, genocide of the Christian inhabitants of the city, approx. 90,000 Christians, all churches destroyed

Jews rebel against the Christians and ally themselves with the Persians, destruction of churches and monasteries, murder |
| 617 AD. | The Persians expel the Jews from Jerusalem and forbid them to enter the city.

The Christians were allowed to rule in Jerusalem again. |
| 632 AD. | Emperor Herakleios: "Doctrine of the newly baptized James", forced baptism, conversion to Christianity, "Israel" back to "Jakub"

Jews flee because they cannot bear the hatred of the Christians. |
636 – 1.099 AD.	**Arab rule**
638 AD.	The Arabs conquer Jerusalem.
	Desurbanization is progressing.
640 AD.	The land of Palestine is conquered by the Arabs.
691 AD.	Muslim Arabs built the Dome of the Rock on the Temple Mount in Jerusalem.
1.098 – 1.291 AD.	**Four crusader states**
	Ideology in defense of the Christian West
	the Kingdom of Jerusalem (1099 - 1291), the County of Edessa (1098 - 1144), the Principality of Antioch (1098 - 1268) and the County of Tripoli (1102 - 1289)

	"Proto-Palestinians", Melkites, Syrian Orthodox and Armenian Apostolic Christians
1.099 – 1.291 AD.	**Kingdom of Jerusalem**
	Latin Kingdom of Jerusalem: rule of the Crusaders, conquest of Jerusalem: massacre of non-Christians
1.244 AD.	Conquest and loss of Jerusalem
1.291 AD.	Siege of the bastion of Acre, conquest of Mamluk, Tyre, Sidon and Beirut
	Post-Philistines: Philistines part of the history of the Arab population in Palestine
1.291 – 1.516 AD.	**Mamluk rule**
	Expulsion of the crusaders
	The castles and towns of the Crusaders were destroyed, the agricultural foundations destroyed, Palestine sparsely populated.
	Military slaves of Central Asian (mostly Turkish) or Eastern European origin, large numbers of Caucasian mercenaries
	Severe economic crisis: tax burdens due to wars, crop failures, famines and plague epidemics
	Gaza was conquered peacefully and was still predominantly Christian at the time of the Crusades. The city was neither destroyed by the Crusaders nor by the Mamelukes.
1.453 AD.	Conquest of Constantinople by the Ottoman Sultan Mehmed II.
	The Turks declared Constantinople, which they called Istanbul, to be their capital.
1.460 AD.	Conquest of Mystras in 1460 AD and of Trebizond in 1461 AD. The old Byzantine Empire merges into Ottoman territory.
1.348 AD.	Pogroms against the Jews in European cities Accusation of well poisoning in order to exterminate the Christians through the plague.
1.349 AD.	Jewish pogrom in Strasbourg, 2.000 victims
1.492 AD.	King Ferdinand II: Jews and Muslims are forced to convert to the Catholic faith. Spain The "golden diaspora" for Jews among Muslims came to an end.
1.497 AD.	King Manuel I: Expulsion of the Jews from Portugal

1.516 – 1.517 AD.	Marj Dabiq: Defeat at Aleppo and the Battle of Raydaniyya outside Cairo
1.517 – 1.917 AD.	**Ottoman rule**
1.517 AD.	the conquest of Jerusalem and Egypt Selim I Ottoman rule in Egypt including Syria and Palestine Agriculture and trade experienced an upswing.
	Under Islamic law, Christians and Jews were granted protected minority status. In Palestine, Christians and Jews had become a vanishing minority. Overall, there has been a sharp decline in the population.
	The population centers are around Jerusalem and Nablus, Galilee and Gaza.
	Palestine also becomes part of the Ottoman Empire and is administered from Istanbul.
	Important trading centers Gaza, Jaffa, Acre, Jerusalem, Nablus and Beersheba
	At the turn of the 16th and 17th centuries, the Ottoman Empire had reached its peak.
1.648/9 AD.	Cossack uprising (insurrection) in Ukraine, massacre of the Ukrainian Jews
1.683 AD.	The Ottoman Empire slowly loses importance
1.690 – 1775 AD.	Bedouin Sheikh Daher el-Omar: Independent local ruler in Palestine, founding of the port city of Haifa From Acre, he ruled over Galilee and later over large parts of Palestine.
1.798 – 99 AD.	Napoleon Bonaparte undertook a campaign to Egypt and Palestine. Gaza and Jaffa (today near Tel-Aviv), Haifa, Nazareth and Tyre, as far as Acre
1.801 AD.	The French withdraw from Egypt and Palestine.
	Pasha and Viceroy of Egypt, Mohammed Ali, gained autonomy for the country on the Nile.
1.819 AD.	Riots and violence against Jews in many cities in Germany and elsewhere in Europe (Amsterdam, Copenhagen, Helsinki, Krakow, smaller towns in Poland, Prague, Graz and Vienna (Hep-Hep riots). [Musa]
1.832 – 1.840 AD.	Muh'd Ali Pasha: rules in Palestine

1.831 AD.	Muhammad Ali Pasha (Egypt) liberated Egypt and Palestine from Ottoman rule.
1.832 AD.	Ibrahim Pasha was able to capture Acre and Damascus in 1832.
1.840 AD.	Egypt had to recognize the sovereignty of the Ottoman Empire over its territory.
	The European powers Great Britain, France, Russia, Austria and Prussia and, from 1871, the German Empire gain economic influence in the Ottoman Empire.
1.841 AD.	The Egyptians completely evacuate the area.
	Beginning of Jewish immigration
1.878 AD.	Foundation of the first moshava Petach Tikva, one of the three types of rural settlements in Israel
	Jews from Eastern Europe increasingly emigrated to Palestine to escape persecution.
1.880 AD.	a wave of anti-Judaism in Europe
1.881 AD.	The assassination of the Russian Tsar Alexander II Nikolayevich
1.881 – 1.884 AD.	The anti-Jewish pogroms in Russia
1.882 AD.	The French Baron Edmond James de Rothschild: He acquires properties in Palestine.
	The first great wave of Zionist immigration.
1.891 AD.	Foundation of the Jewish Colonisation Association JCA
1.896 – now	**Zionism**
1.896 AD.	The Viennese journalist Dr. Theodor Herzl: "The Jewish State", the spiritual basis of political Zionism all attempts at assimilation by the Jews failed in principle; they always remained foreigners Herzl: the prophet of the Jewish state
1.896 AD.	The emergence of Christian Zionism
	"insidious Jewish quest for world domination" "The Protocols of the Elders of Zion: The Program of the International Secret Government", since the beginning of the 20th century
	The idea of pan-Islamism and pan-Arabism to strengthen Arab identity. Pan-Islamism: the unity of all Muslims in an Islamic state or caliphate. Pan-Arabism: to strengthen the Arab-Islamic identity

	Pan-Semitism: Jews and Arabs, both so-called Semitic peoples, to connect
	Tensions between the Arabs living in Palestine and the immigrant Jews increased.
1.897 AD.	1st Zionist Congress to escape anti-Semitism; in addition to Palestine, over 30 other options were discussed
1.900 AD.	500,000 rather poor people inhabited the narrow coastal strip, 26,000 Jews
1.901 AD.	Jewish National Fund: Land acquisition in Palestine, landless Arab farmers lose their livelihoods Jewish land purchase companies acquired land. Tel Aviv was founded in 1909 as the "first Jewish city".
	Israeli-Palestinian conflict: social conflict between the Arab rural population and Jewish settlers
1.882 – 1.903 AD.	1st Aliyah: First Zionist immigration (Aliyah) from Russia to Palestine: 20,000 - 30,000
	The land was bought with money, but landless and dispossessed Arabs lived there.
1.905 – 1.914 AD.	2nd Aliyah: from Russia: 35,000 - 40,000
	60,000 Jews in Palestine
1.916 AD.	The Arab Revolt with the participation of T. E. Lawrence against the Ottoman Sultan.
1.916 AD.	Sykes-Picot Agreement: British Palestine and Iraq, French Lebanon and Syria
1.917 AD.	The Holy City of Jerusalem was conquered by Britten in December 1917.
1.917 AD.	Balfour Declaration: "National home for the Jewish people in Palestine" Commitment to the establishment of a national homeland for the Jews in Palestine after 2000 years of the dream of a Jewish state At the same time an Arab state with Palestine, i.e. 2 states on one territory!
1.917 AD.	British troops advance from Egypt into Palestine and take Jerusalem in December 1917.
1.918 AD.	In September 1918, the Ottoman front in Palestine collapsed.
1.918 AD.	However, the fighting in Palestine and Jordan dragged on until 1918.
1.918 – 1.948 AD.	**British rule**
1.918 AD.	Laying of the foundation stone of the Hebrew University of Jerusalem

1.918 AD.	"Palestine" administrative district
1.919 AD.	Faisal-Weizmann Agreement: common ancestry of the Jews and Arabs of Palestine
1.919 – 1.923 AD.	3rd Aliyah: Soviet Union and Poland: approx. 35,000
1.920 AD.	Nabi Musa riots: anti-Jewish riots in the Old City of Jerusalem on April 4, 1920
1.920 AD.	Palestine including Transjordan and Mesopotamia as Iraq British League of Nations mandate
1.924 – 1.931 AD.	4th Aliyah: Poland and Soviet Union: approx. 80,000
1.925 AD.	Inauguration of the Hebrew University of Jerusalem
1.926 AD.	1st Islamic Congress chaired by the Saudi Arabian King Abd al-Aziz ibn Saud in Mecca
1.931 AD.	General Islamic Congress in Jerusalem
1.932 – 1.938 AD.	5th Aliyah: Poland, Germany: approx. 200,000
1.933 AD.	Adolf Hitler was appointed German Reich Chancellor by Reich President Paul von Hindenburg on January 30, 1933.
1.935 AD.	radical preacher Sheikh Izzedin al-Kassam: Palestinians call for jihad against the British Mandate and Jews
1.936 AD.	Arab revolt: peaceful coexistence between the two population groups is impossible, Mohammed Amin al-Husseini
1.937 AD.	"We will drive out the Arabs and take their place." Ben Gurion's letter to his son Ben Gurion: Prime Minister of Israel in 1948 – 1953, 1955 - 1963
1.938 AD.	from November 9 to 10, 1938, also known as Kristallnacht or Reichskristallnacht
1.939 – 1.945 AD.	6th Aliyah: Poland, Germany, Romania, Hungary, Czechoslovakia: approx. 80,000
1.939 AD.	British White Paper: Palestine should not become a Jewish state the establishment of an independent Palestinian state within ten years Jewish immigration in five years: Number of Jewish immigrants max. 1/3 of the total population of the country So 75,000 Jewish immigrants in five years
1.939 – 1.945 AD.	From September 1, 1939 to September 2, 1945: the second global war waged by all the major powers

1.941 – 1.945 AD.	The Holocaust ('completely burnt') or the Shoah ('the catastrophe', 'the great misfortune/disaster')
1.942 AD.	The "Discussion on the Final Solution of the Jewish Question", Adolf Eichmann, on 20.01.1942, Villa "Am Großen Wannsee Nr:56/58"
1.944 – 1.948 AD.	Bricha "Escape": 250,000 people Eastern Europe, Poland, Hungary, Czechoslovakia, Romania, Yugoslavia and the Soviet Union
1.943 n. Chr	The uprising in the Warsaw Ghetto on April 19, 1943, against the German occupying forces
1.945 n. Chr	Foundation of the Arab League in Cairo and start of the boycott of Israel by the Arab League
1.946 – 1.948 AD.	7th Aliyah: Poland, Romania: approx. 56,000
1.947 AD.	UN Resolution 181: 609,000 Jews in Palestine -> 55% of the land; 1.38 million Arabs in Palestine -> 42% of the land The Arab states, the Arab League and the Palestinian Arab High Committee reject partition.
1.947 – 1.949 AD.	**The Nakba** (misfortune, catastrophe): Flight and expulsion of approx. 700,000 Arab Palestinians
	300,000 (area under Jordanian control), 230,000 (area under Egyptian control), in other neighboring countries

	After that, only 150,000 Arabs left in Palestine	
		1.5 million Arabs with refugee status UN Resolution 181: Partition of Palestine into an Arab and a Jewish state UN Resolution 181: Two-state solution an Arab state and a Jewish state
1.947 AD.		

Due to the immigration of Jews from Europe, the number of Jewish inhabitants in Palestine increased very quickly.

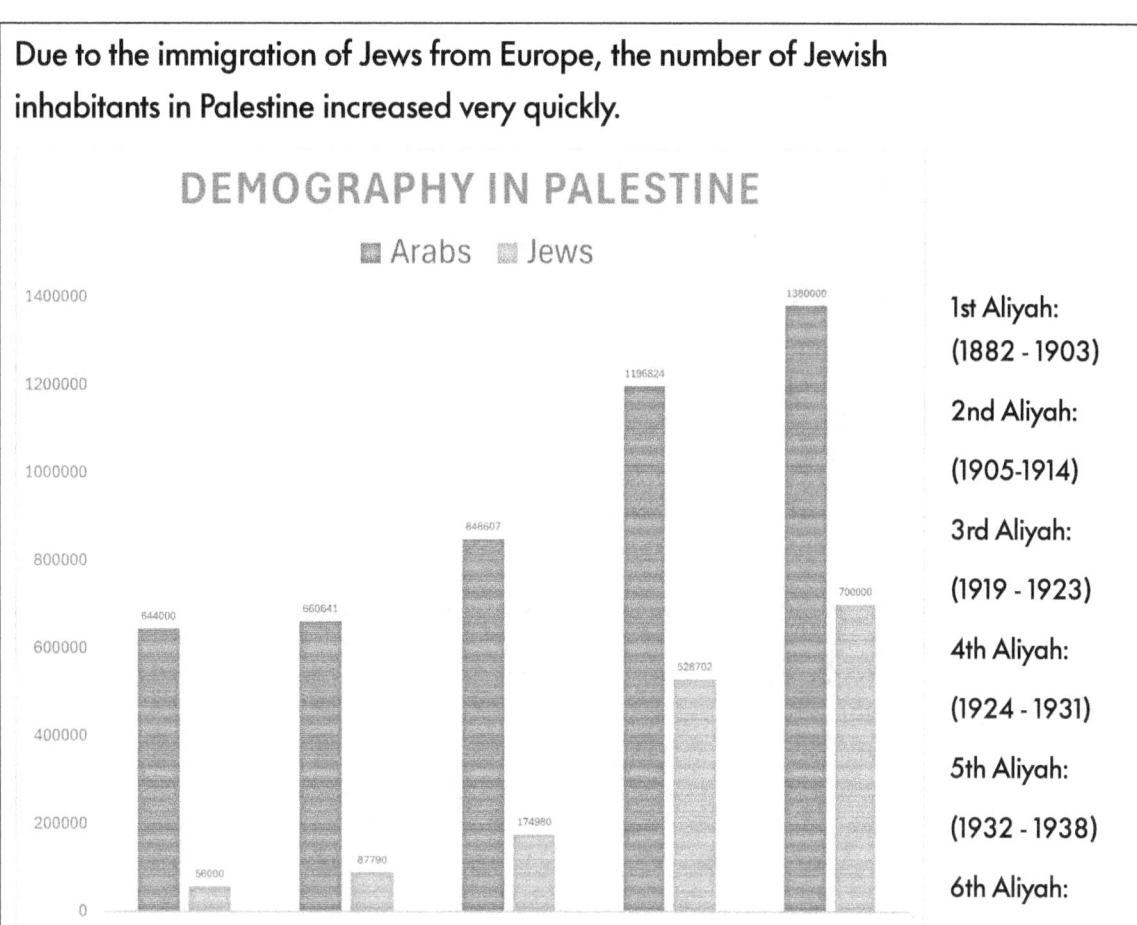

DEMOGRAPHY IN PALESTINE

■ Arabs ■ Jews

1st Aliyah: (1882 - 1903)

2nd Aliyah: (1905-1914)

3rd Aliyah: (1919 - 1923)

4th Aliyah: (1924 - 1931)

5th Aliyah: (1932 - 1938)

6th Aliyah: (1939 - 1945)

7th Aliyah: (1946 - 1948)

1.948 AD.	**State of Israel**
	After 2670 years: Kingdom of Israel! End of the British Mandate (May 14), proclamation of the State of Israel (May 15), Tel Aviv as capital city
	Declaration of Independence: The Jewish people came into being in the land of Israel. Jewish homelessness, Holocaust, persecution of the Jews It will be based on freedom, justice, equality and peace in the spirit of the visions of the prophets of Israel.
	"ERETZ-ISRAEL [(Hebrew) - the Land of Israel, Palestine], was the birthplace of the Jewish people. Here their spiritual, religious and political identity was shaped." "Jews strove in every successive generation to re-establish themselves in their ancient homeland." "Here they first attained to statehood, created cultural values of national and universal significance and gave to the world the eternal Book of Books."

	"the people kept faith with it throughout their Dispersion and never ceased to pray and hope for their return to it" "In the year 5657 (1897), at the summons of the spiritual father of the Jewish State, Theodore Herzl, the First Zionist Congress." Tel Aviv, May 14, 1948
1.948 – 1.949 AD.	1st Middle East War (May 15): Egypt, Transjordan, Syria, Lebanon and Iraq, expansion of territory by 23%.
	400 Arab villages and over 100 hamlets destroyed, Arab armies destroyed Jewish settlements and kibbutzim Mandate Palestine disappears from the political map.
	Palestinians on Israeli territory: "Israeli Arabs", "48 Arabs", "Palestinians with Israeli citizenship"
	The expulsion of the Palestinians from Lydda and Ramle
	1,000,000 Jews who fled from Arab countries, 850,000 refugees in Israel, "forgotten millions"
1.950 AD.	The Israeli government declares Jerusalem the capital of the State of Israel.
1.948 – 1.951 AD.	Mass Jewish immigration from Arab countries, Poland and Romania
1.955 – 1.957 AD.	Immigration of Jews from North Africa
1.956 AD.	2nd Middle East War between Egypt and Great Britain, France and Israel (Sinai campaign)
1.959 AD.	Fatah, "opening, opening, liberating; (removing obstacles)", cf. futūh.
1.962 AD.	Adolf Eichmann trial and death penalty (Holocaust)
1.964 AD.	Foundation of the Palestine Liberation Organization (PLO)
1.967 AD.	3rd Middle East War Six-Day War: Egypt, Syria and Jordan, Six-Day War, Jerusalem reunited
	3 No's: No to peace with Israel, No to recognition of Israel, No to negotiations with Israel -> Rejection
1.973 AD.	4th Middle East War ("Yom Kippur War") Israel against Egypt and Syria
1.979 AD.	The peace treaty between Israel and Egypt

1.975 AD.	Zionism as "a form of racism" by Arab states, Eastern Bloc states and some Third World states
1.978 AD.	1st World Conference against Racism, Geneva
1.982 AD.	5th Middle East War: Start of the Lebanon War (Operation Peace for Galilea)
1.983 AD.	2nd World Conference against Racism, Geneva
1.984 – 1.985 AD.	Operation Moses - the resettlement of Ethiopian Jews to Israel
1.987 AD.	**Foundation of Hamas**
	Hamas' of the movement's full name, Harakat al-Muqawama al-Islamijja, which means 'Islamic Resistance Movement', means 'zeal' or 'enthusiasm'.
	"Israel will come into being and continue to exist until Islam abolishes it, just as it abolished what came before it." The imam and martyr Hassan al-Banna
	Israel's right to exist is called into question. Fight against a postulated "Zionist invasion": all Muslims and Arabs, liberation of Palestine "Israel challenges Islam and Muslims through its Jewish character and its Jewish inhabitants."
	Hamas Charter: This is the Charter of the Islamic Resistance Movement Artikel 1: The Islamic Resistance Movement: The Movement's programme is Islam. Artikel 3: The basic structure of the Islamic Resistance Movement consists of Moslems Artikel 6: The Islamic Resistance Movement is a distinguished Palestinian movement, whose allegiance is to Allah, and whose way of life is Islam. Artikel 8: Allah is its target, the Prophet is its model, the Koran its constitution: Jihad is its path and death for the sake of Allah is the loftiest of its wishes. Artikel 11: The Islamic Resistance Movement believes that the land of Palestine is an Islamic Waqf consecrated for future Moslem generations until Judgement Day. Palestine is an Islamic Waqf land consecrated for Moslem generations until Judgement Day. Artikel 12: Nationalism, from the point of view of the Islamic Resistance Movement, is part of the religious creed.

Artikel 13: Abusing any part of Palestine is abuse directed against part of religion.

There is no solution for the Palestinian question except through Jihad.

Artikel 15: The day that enemies usurp part of Moslem land, Jihad becomes the individual duty of every Moslem.

Artikel 16: It is necessary to follow Islamic orientation in educating the Islamic generations in our region by teaching the religious duties, comprehensive study of the Koran, the study of the Prophet's Sunna (his sayings and doings) and learning about Islamic history and heritage from their authentic sources.

Artikel 17: The Moslem woman has a role no less important than that of the moslem man in the battle of liberation.

Artikel 20: Moslem society is a mutually responsible society.

In their Nazi treatment, the Jews made no exception for women or children. They attack people where their breadwinning is concerned, extorting their money and threatening their honour. Deportation from the homeland is a kind of murder.

Artikel 22: The imperialistic forces in the Capitalist West and Communist East, support the enemy with all their might, in money and in men. These forces take turns in doing that. The day Islam appears, the forces of infidelity would unite to challenge it, for the infidels are of one nation.

Artikel 32: World Zionism, together with imperialistic powers, try through a studied plan and an intelligent strategy to remove one Arab state after another from the circle of struggle against Zionism, in order to have it finally face the Palestinian people only.

Today it is Palestine, tomorrow it will be one country or another. The Zionist plan is limitless. After Palestine, the Zionists aspire to expand from the Nile to the Euphrates.

Artikel 34: Palestine is the navel of the globe and the crossroad of the continents. Since the dawn of history, it has been the target of expansionists.

Thus it was that the Crusaders came with their armies, bringing with them their creed and carrying their Cross. They were able to defeat the Moslems for a while, but the Moslems were able to retrieve the land only when they stood under the wing of their religious banner.

"Say to those who disbelieve, "You will be defeated, and rounded up into Hell—an awful resting-place." Sure 3:12

Artikel 34: A creed could not be fought except by a creed, and in the last analysis, victory is for the just, for justice is certainly victorious.

Artikel 35: The defeat of the Crusaders at the hands of Salah ed-Din al-Ayyubi and the rescuing of Palestine from their hands, as well as the defeat of the Tatars at Ein Galot,

	breaking their power at the hands of Qataz and Al-Dhaher Bivers and saving the Arab world from the Tatar onslaught which aimed at the destruction of every meaning of human civilization. The Movement draws lessons and examples from all this. Artikel 36: The Islamic Resistance Movement adopts Islam as its way of life. Islam is its creed and religion. The last of our prayers will be praise to Allah, the Master of the Universe.
	"Palestine is an Arab-Islamic country." [Charta 2017]
	"The Zionist project is a racist, aggressive, colonial and expansionist project based on the appropriation of the property of others" [Charta 2017]
	"The establishment of "Israel" is completely illegal and violates the inalienable rights of the Palestinian people and against their will and the will of the Ummah;" [Charta 2017]
	"The Islamic resistance movement is a link in the chain of jihad against the Zionist invasion." [Charta 2017]
	"The Palestinian question can only be solved through jihad. Initiatives, proposals and international conferences are a pointless waste of time, a sacrilegious game, ..." [Charta 2017]
	"because Palestine is Islamic soil." [Charta 2017]
	"In Palestine lies the first of the two directions of prayer and the third holiest site of Islam, the destination of the Prophet Mohammad's nightly journey to heaven" [Charta 2017]
	"Leaving the conflict with Zionism is high treason, and whoever commits it is cursed." [Charta 2017]
	"The Islamic Resistance Movement sees itself as the spearhead in the confrontation with world Zionism," [Charta 2017]
1.987 AD.	1st Intifada: "Shaking off", uprising against Hamas
1.988 AD.	Proclamation of the State of Palestine by the PLO
1.989 AD.	Start of mass immigration from the Soviet Union to Israel
1.992 AD.	Diplomatic relations with China and India
1.992 AD.	Founding of the Qassam Brigades: military sub-organization of the Palestinian Islamist terrorist organization Hamas
1.993 AD.	Oslo I: Creation of the Palestinian Authority in place of the Israeli military administration the PLO recognized Israel's right to exist

	Israel accepts the PLO as the legitimate representative of all Palestinians
1.993 AD.	Hamas begins suicide attacks in Israel
1.994 AD.	Gaza-Jericho Agreement of the Palestinian Authority in the Gaza Strip and Jericho Area
1.994 AD.	Establishment of the Palestinian Authority and the Palestinian Authority Security Service
1.995 AD.	Oslo II: Expansion of Palestinian self-government implemented in the West Bank and Gaza Strip
1.996 AD.	Operation Grapes of Wrath
1.997 AD.	Hebron Protocol, signed by Israel and the Palestinian Authority
2.000 AD.	Israeli-Palestinian negotiations at Camp David
2.000 AD.	Visit by Pope Paul II.
2.000 AD.	2nd Intifada
2.001 AD.	2nd World Conference against Racism in Durban (South Africa) turns into an anti-Semitic rally
2.002 AD.	Operation Defensive Shield for the reoccupation of almost all autonomous areas
2.002 AD.	The anti-terror fence
2.004 AD.	Operation Rainbow by the Israeli army in the Gaza Strip.
2.004 AD.	Gaza operation "Days of Atonement"
2.005 AD.	The Israeli army evacuates all Jewish settlements in the Gaza Strip.
2.005 AD.	First BDS Israeli Apartheid Week
2.005 AD.	Disengagement plan: Israel evacuates all settlements in the Gaza Strip and four settlements in the northern West Bank
2.006 AD.	International Holocaust Cartoon Competition in Tehran (Iran)

2.006 AD.	Conference on Holocaust denial in Tehran
2.006 AD.	Start of the Fatah-Hamas conflict, Palestinian civil war or fratricidal conflict
2.007 AD.	Hamas violently takes power in the Gaza Strip: Hamas' declared goal is the destruction of the state of Israel.
	Israel declares Gaza a "hostile territory" after violent takeover of the Gaza Strip by Hamas
2.008 AD.	Cast Lead, 10,000 rockets and mortar shells from the Gaza Strip
2.008 AD.	Israel invades the Gaza Strip.
2.008 AD.	UN Resolution 1850: Roadmap for a lasting two-state solution to settle the Israeli-Palestinian conflict
2.008 – 2.009 AD.	Operation Cast Lead: air strikes on targets in the Gaza Strip
2.009 AD.	UN Resolution 1860: immediate, permanent, respected ceasefire, withdrawal of Israeli forces from Gaza Israeli-Palestinian peace solution, two democratic states, Israel and Palestine, living side by side in peace
2.011 AD.	Film: Valley of the Wolves - Palestine, anti-Semitic content, propaganda film
2.011 AD.	Prawer Plan: Expulsion and resettlement of 40,000 to 70,000 Palestinians - Bedouins in the Naqab/Negev - from their villages
2.013 AD.	Palestinian President Mahmoud Abbas: "State of Palestine" instead of "Palestinian Authority" in official communications
2.014 AD.	The Israeli army's Operation Protective Edge in the Gaza Strip.
2.016 AD.	2nd Holocaust cartoon competition in Tehran
2.016 AD.	UN Resolution 2334: Israeli settlements have no legal validity, a blatant violation of international law
2.017 AD.	US President Donald Trump recognizes Jerusalem as the capital of Israel.
2.017 AD.	Film: Valley of the Wolves - Fatherland, anti-Semitism

2.017 AD.	OIC Special Summit in Istanbul
2.018 AD.	Israel celebrates the 70th anniversary of its founding
2.018 AD.	"Great March of Return", massive protests along the border between the Gaza Strip and Israel
2.019 AD.	US President Donald Trump: Recognition of the Syrian Golan Heights annexed by Israel as Israeli territory
2.019 AD.	Mahmud Abbas: "This land belongs to its people, its inhabitants and the Canaanites who were here 5,000 years ago - and we are the Canaanites!" (no evidence)
2.020 AD.	Peace agreement (Abraham Accords): United Arab Emirates, Bahrain, Sudan and Morocco
2.021 AD.	Israel-Gaza conflict 2021: 48 Palestinians (including 66 children) and 13 Israelis killed
2.021 AD.	Conflict with Hamas: eleven-day armed conflict between Israel and Hamas, East Jerusalem
2.022 AD.	Operation Breaking Dawn: Military operation launched against targets in the Gaza Strip and West Bank
2.023 AD.	The al-Aqsa conflicts: Palestinian worshippers and Israeli police officers at the al-Aqsa Mosque in Jerusalem
2.023 AD.	The Israeli air strikes on the Gaza Strip, Operation Shield and Arrow
2.023 AD.	**Operation Al-Aqsa Flood**: October 7, Hamas terror attack on Israel, 1139 dead, 5400 injured, 240 hostages
2.023 – 2.024 AD.	Military operation "Iron Swords" massive air strikes and a ground offensive the high number of civilian casualties Catastrophic situation in the Gaza Strip Gaza Strip cut off and isolated Gaza Strip is like a ghetto and a war zone
	an armed conflict between the State of Israel and Hamas
2.023	9. Oktober 2023: Complete blockade of the Gaza Strip
2.023 AD.	from 27 to 28 October 2023: Ground offensive in the north of the Gaza Strip
	Is the Israeli army committing genocide in Gaza?

	The supply of electricity, drinking water, food and fuel was cut off. How far can revenge and retribution go?
2.023 – 2.024 AD.	Global tsunami of anti-Semitism: social media, universities, cafés, grocery stores, demonstrations, clubs, events, internet, schools
2.024 AD.	Statista (April 09, 2024): 33,207 dead in Gaza, approx. 75,933 injured In the West Bank: 428 Palestinian dead and around 4,760 injured
Problems	
Politics	One-state solution, two-state solution as a solution to the Israeli-Palestinian conflict, three-state solution
Zionism	the attempt to expand the territory of Israel as a colonialist power and to expel the Palestinians.
Neo-Zionism	Settlement of the occupied territories in the West Bank
Refugees	The United Nations Relief and Works Agency for Palestine Refugees in the Near East (UNRWA) estimates that there are currently around 5 million registered Arab Palestinian refugees in the region.
Islamic world	Aggressors, "Zionist entity", "Zionist occupation"
Conflict	Synagogue, church and mosque Torah, Gospel and Koran God: omnipotent, omniscient, all-good (for all three) YHWH, Vater, Sohn, Ghost and Allah David Star, Cross and Crescent moon Moses, Jesus and Mohammed Abraham: Isaac (Jews), Isaac (Christians) and Ishmael (Muslims) The 613 prohibitions and bans, faith in Jesus Christ and grace, the five pillars of Islam kippah, schtreimel, fish icon, taqiyah, turban and headscarf kittel, hite robe-like garment, argeneshe smock, tefillin, tallit or able, gown, rasson, phelonion or thobe, jubba, kandura Yom Kippur, Easter and Good Friday or Ramadan, Eid al-Fitr, Eid al-Adha

Capital city	Jerusalem: Temple Mount (Wailing Wall), Golgotha, the al-Aqsa Mosque

Sources

Łukasz Niesiołowski-Spanò, Krystyna Stebnicka: Historia Zydow w starozytnosci - Od Thotmesa do Mahometa, Wydawnictwo Naukowe PWN SA, Warszawa 2020.

Łukasz Niesiołowski-Spanò: Początki Izraela i Izraelitów, Uniwersytet Warszawski, 2022.

https://de.wikipedia.org/wiki/Seevölker

https://www.jewiki.net/wiki/Zeittafel_zur_jüdischen_Geschichte

https://www.bpb.de/shop/zeitschriften/izpb/israel-336/268928/zeittafel/

https://de.wikipedia.org/wiki/Mamluken#Mamluken_in_Ägypten

Die Geschichte Israels und Palästinas - erf.de

https://www.erf.de/lesen/themen/gesellschaft/die-geschichte-des-nahostkonflikts/2270-542-7670

https://www.bpb.de/shop/zeitschriften/izpb/israel-336/268894/die-beziehungen-zwischen-israelis-und-palaestinensern/

https://de.wikipedia.org/wiki/Geschichte_der_Philister

https://de.wikipedia.org/wiki/Philister

https://rainer-langlitz.de/blog/?wem-gehoert-palaestina-eine-zeitliche-darstellung-von-konflikten,-kaempfen-und-kriegen-um-eine-beanspruchte-region

https://www.erf.de/lesen/themen/gesellschaft/die-geschichte-israels-und-palaestinas/2270-542-7666

https://de.wikipedia.org/wiki/Chronologie_des_israelisch-palästinensischen_Konflikts

Holy Bible, New International Reader's Version®, NIrV® (Anglicised)Copyright © 1995, 1996, 1998, 2014 by Biblica

https://de.wikipedia.org/wiki/Geschichte_der_arabischen_Bevölkerung_in_Palästina

https://www.israel-spezialist.de/heiliges-land/geschichte-heiliges-land/osmanische-herrschaft.htm

https://www.worldhistory.org/trans/de/1-192/palastina/

ENCYCLOPAEDIA JUDAICA, Second Edition, Keter Publishing House Ltd., 2007, Seite 11804 ff, Seite 7217 ff, Seite 5334 ff

Hadhrat Mirza Masroor Ahmad: KORAN, DER HEILIGE QUR'AN, Arabisch mit deutscher Dbersetzung, Islam International Publications Ltd., 2021, Verlag Der Islam

Den geheimnisvollen Philistern auf der Spur: www.wissenschaft.de/geschichte-archaeologie/den-geheimnisvollen-philistern-auf-der-spur/, 3. Juli 2019

Hamas Covenant 1988: The Covenant of the Islamic Resistance Movement. 18 August 1988, https://avalon.law.yale.edu/20th_century/hamas.asp

[Charta 2017] Die Charta der Hamas von 1988 und 2017 im Wortlaut - ins Deutsche übersetzt, https://www.kritiknetz.de/images/stories/texte/charta der hamas.pdf, Hrsg. Heinz Gess, ISSN 1866-4105, 2023

Talal Itani: The Quran. Translated to English by Talal Itani, Published by ClearQuran, Dallas, Beirut, 2009-2012
Talal A. Itani

Eigene Schrift der Philister entdeckt? 16.03.2007, https://www.spektrum.de/news/eigene-schrift-der-philister-entdeckt/868489

Palästina: 25 Oktober 2018, https://www.worldhistory.org/trans/de/1-192/palastina/

DAGON: Watch Tower Bible and Tract Society of Pennsylvania, 2024, https://wol.jw.org/de/wol/d/r10/lp-x/1200001107

Carl S. Ehrlich: Die Philister und ihr Kult, 2007, file: Die_Philister_und_ihr_Kult_2008.pdf

Christian Frevel: Wo und wann lernt Israel seinen Gott kennen?, Religionsgeschichte: JHWH und der Exodus, Welt und Umwelt der Bibel 2/19

J. Wellhausen: Israelitische und Jüdische Geschichte, 10. Auflage, Berlin 2004, 23

PETER SANDMEYER, KENNETH GARRETT: Heiliges Land: Wiege der Verheißung, National Geographic, Heft 12 / 2014, Seiten 44 bis 63

https://de.wikipedia.org/wiki/Auge_für_Auge

Dr. Izzeddin Musa: Die Geschichte Palästinas von 600.000 Jahre v. Chr. bis 2008 n. Chr.: http://www.felastini.com/index.php/ar/information/national-information/10270-geschichte-palaestinas

[Ur] Urgeschichte Palästinas: wiki, https://de.wikipedia.org/wiki/Urgeschichte_Palästinas

[br] britannica.com

[Veen] Peter G. van der Veen und Wolfgang Zwickel: Die neue Israel-Inschrift und ihre historischen Implikationen, „Vom Leben umfangen" - Ägypten, das Alte Testament und das Gespräch der Religionen, Gedenkschrift für Manfred Görg, 2014 Ugarit-Verlag, Münster.

Great migration in Palestine

What	From	Until	King	Persons
Exodus from Egypt	1.500 BC.			
Taking of the land of	1.500 BC.	1.300	Joshua	
Exil, Deportation	734 BC.		Tiglath-Pileser III	13,250 people from Israel
Exil, Deportation	722 BC.		Tiglath-Pileser III	27,290 people
Exil, Deportation	701 BC.		Sennacherib	
Babylonian captivity	586 BC.	538 BC.	Nebuchadnezzar	
Returning	539 BC.	529 BC.	Cyrus II of Persia	
Returning	521 BC.	515 BC.		
Returning	465 BC.	424 BC.		
Exil, Diaspora	70 AD.			Great Jewish War, Jerusalem destroyed by the Romans
Exil, Diaspora	135 AD.			Bar-Kochba, Judea renamed Syria Palestine
Byzantine rule	500 AD.			90% Christians, 10% Jews in Palestine
Zionism	1.897 AD.			
1st Aliyah	1.882 AD.	1.903		20,000 - 30,000
2nd Aliyah	1.905 AD.	1.914		35,000 - 40,000
3rd Aliyah	1.919 AD.	1.923		35,000
4th Aliyah	1.924 AD.	1.931		80,000
5th Aliyah	1.932 AD.	1.938		200,000
6th Aliyah	1.939 AD.	1.945		80,000
7th Aliyah	1.946 AD.	1.948		56,000
The Nakba	1.947 AD.	1.949		700,000 Arab Palestinians
"Forgotten millions"	1.948 AD.	1.949		1,000,000 Jews who fled from Arab countries, 850,000 refugees in Israel, "forgotten millions"
Immigration	1.955 AD.	1.957		Immigration of Jews from North Africa

Emblem of Israel

Coat of arms of Jerusalem

Coat of arms of Jerusalem

Crown of Thorns

Coat of arms of Palestine

Sources

Cover page: © NASA's Goddard Space Flight Center, Visible Earth is part of the EOS Project Science Office at NASA Goddard Space Flight Center,

MiddleEast tmo 2013349 lrg.jpg, sattelite image of snow in the Middle East, 15.12.2013.

Hamas fights against the state of Israel

Neither side has exclusive rights

to this city.

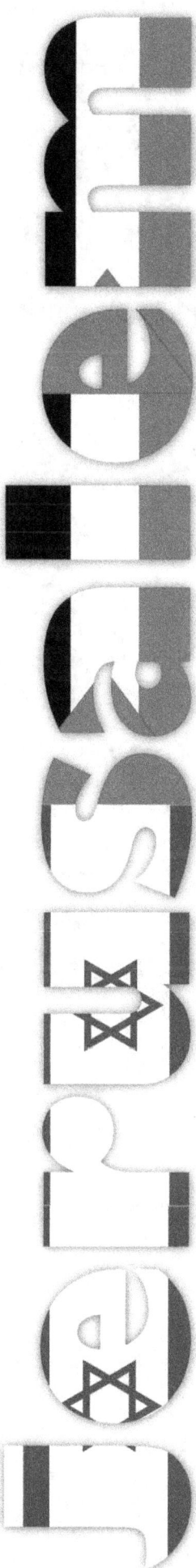